CAN GLOBALIZATION PROMOTE HUMAN RIGHTS?

ESSAYS ON HUMAN RIGHTS

EDITED BY THOMAS CUSHMAN

This series features important new works by leading figures in the interdisciplinary field of human rights. Books in the series present provocative and powerful statements, theories, or views on contemporary issues in human rights. The aim of the series is to provide short, accessible works that will present new and original thinking in crystalline form and in a language accessible to a wide range of scholars, policymakers, students, and general readers. The series will include works by anthropologists, sociologists, philosophers, political scientists, and those working in the more traditional fields of human rights, including practitioners.

Thomas Cushman is Professor of Sociology at Wellesley College. He previously edited a series for The Pennsylvania State University Press titled Post-Communist Cultural Studies, in which a dozen volumes appeared. He is the founding editor of two journals, *Human Rights Review* and the *Journal of Human Rights*, and he now serves as Editor-at-Large for the latter. He is a Fellow of the Yale Center for Cultural Sociology.

ALREADY PUBLISHED:

Bryan Turner, *Vulnerability and Human Rights* (2004)

Keith Tester, *Humanitarianism and Modern Culture* (2010)

OTHER TITLES FORTHCOMING:

John Rodden, *Dialectics, Dogmas, and Dissent: Stories from East German Victims of Human Rights Abuse* (2010)

Daniel Levy and Natan Sznaider, *Human Rights and Memory*

Nancy Tuana, *Global Climate Change and Human Rights*

RHODA E. HOWARD-HASSMANN

CAN
GLOBALIZATION
PROMOTE
HUMAN
RIGHTS?

THE PENNSYLVANIA STATE UNIVERSITY PRESS
UNIVERSITY PARK, PENNSYLVANIA

Library of Congress Cataloging-in-Publication Data
Howard-Hassmann, Rhoda E., 1948–

    Can globalization promote human rights? /
    Rhoda E. Howard-Hassmann.

        p.   cm. — (Essays on human rights)
Includes bibliographical references and index.
Summary: "An examination of globalization's effects on human
rights, world poverty, and inequality. Describes international
human rights law and the international social movement for
reform of globalization"—Provided by publisher.
ISBN 978-0-271-03739-4 (cloth: alk. paper)
1. Globalization.
2. Human rights and globalization.
3. Globalization—Moral and ethical aspects.
I. Title.

HF1359.H69   2010
323—dc22
2009047838

The Pennsylvania State University Press is a member of the
Association of American University Presses.

It is the policy of The Pennsylvania State University Press to
use acid-free paper. Publications on uncoated stock satisfy the
minimum requirements of American National Standard for
Information Sciences—Permanence of Paper for Printed Library
Material, ANSI Z39.48–1992.

This book is printed on Natures Natural, which contains 50%
post-consumer waste.

In memory of my colleague and friend
Katarina Tomasevski, 1953–2006

United Nations Special Rapporteur on the Right to Education,
1998–2004

brilliant, beautiful, bold, and brave

extraordinarily generous

and extraordinarily dedicated to human rights

for which she gave her life.

CONTENTS

ACKNOWLEDGMENTS

Many people at Wilfrid Laurier University in Waterloo, Ontario, where I hold the Canada Research Chair in International Human Rights, assisted me during the completion of this book. Sue Horton and Christine Neill of the Department of Economics were extraordinarily generous in helping me make sense of the data in chapter 2. Ali Zaidi of the Department of Global Studies carefully commented on chapter 8. I worked through several drafts of the manuscript while teaching graduate students from the Department of Political Science, Department of Sociology, Department of Religion and Culture, Master's in International Public Policy, and PhD in Global Governance in two courses in 2008. Jay Allingham, Meghan Bateman, Michael Bittle, Giovanni Congi, Robert Cundari, Jackie DaSilva, Nicole Desmarais, Jacqueline Flatt, Matthew Foster, Sadira Garfinkel, Lyndsay Hockin, Richard Kirkham, Tiffany Kizito, Matthew Overall, Jelena Popovic, Natalie Ravoi, Kirsten Pries, Stephanie Ryan, Leah Sarson, Kris Slater, Samantha Sue Ping, Lindsay Walden, and Craig Wood all contributed useful ideas and comments, while J. Ricardo Tranjan offered trenchant criticisms and led a three-hour discussion of an early version of the manuscript. Anastasi Bakolias, Stefanie Bujnowski, Keith Calow, Gregory Eady, James Gaede, Michael Lisetto-Smith, Matthew Overall, and Rena Patel provided valuable research assistance, responding promptly and cheerfully to my many requests for information.

Wendy Webb, administrative assistant to the chair, once again kept budgets, paychecks, and many other details under control so that I could devote my time to writing. Wendy's warmth, efficiency, and loyalty have been integral to all my research for the past six years. I am most grateful to the Canada Research Chairs Program for the position I hold at Laurier, which gave me the resources and time I needed to work on this manuscript, and I am certainly grateful to Wilfrid Laurier University itself.

Michael Freeman of the University of Essex commented thoroughly on an early version of chapter 2, as did Don Wells of McMaster University on an early version of chapter 6; Peter Baehr also offered critical feedback on a related work. My beloved friend Grace Stewart generously read the entire manuscript, commenting on it from her dual point of view as a teacher of English grammar and an interested citizen. My friend of forty years' standing, Anne Castle, formerly of the World Bank, carefully read and critiqued chapters 1 through 6. Will Coleman, now a colleague in the Balsillie School of International Affairs in Waterloo, Ontario, was there at the beginning, when the idea for the article that eventually became this book germinated at an interdisciplinary conference on globalization and autonomy that he organized at McMaster University in 2002. Anthony Lombardo, my research assistant at the time, was also extremely helpful.

Sandy Thatcher of The Pennsylvania State University Press was extremely supportive throughout the production of this book, as was Tom Cushman, editor of the Press's series Essays on Human Rights. I was pleased and encouraged by the review submitted by my esteemed colleague, Gavin Kitching, and found the other (anonymous) review of the manuscript useful. I am also most grateful to Julie Schoelles for her superb editing.

Parts of this book draw on two earlier articles I wrote on human rights and globalization: "The Second Great Transformation: Human Rights Leapfrogging in the Era of Globalization," *Human Rights Quarterly* 27, no. 1 (2005): 1–40, and "Culture, Human Rights, and the Politics of Resentment in the Era of Globalization," *Human Rights Review* 6, no. 1 (2004): 5–26. I am extremely grateful to Bert Lockwood, editor of *Human Rights Quarterly*, for his interest in "The Second Great Transformation" and his long-standing regard for my work. Richard Claude, founding editor of *Human Rights Quarterly*, also encouraged publication of the article. I express my appreciation to Gary Herbert, editor of *Human Rights Review*, for publishing the second article. I thank both *Human Rights Quarterly* and *Human Rights Review* for permission to use material from the two articles in this volume.

Finally, I thank my husband, Peter McCabe, an economist by trade. He was extraordinarily patient with me as I worked through the economic background for this book, but more than that, had I not lived with him for the past thirty-one years I would not have been able to write it at all. His critical comments and insightful observations have influenced all my thinking since the day we met in December 1976.

Rhoda E. Howard-Hassmann

ACRONYMS

AI	Amnesty International
CSR	corporate social responsibility
DFI	direct foreign investment
EPZ	export processing zone
GDP	gross domestic product
GNI	gross national income
GNP	gross national product
HRNGO	human rights nongovernmental organization
HRW	Human Rights Watch
ICCPR	International Covenant on Civil and Political Rights
ICESCR	International Covenant on Economic, Social, and Cultural Rights
IFI	international financial institution
ILO	International Labor Organization
IMF	International Monetary Fund
IO	international organization
NGO	nongovernmental organization
NIEO	New International Economic Order
PPP	purchasing power parity
PQLI	physical quality of life index
PRSP	Poverty Reduction Strategy Paper

SAP	structural adjustment program
SOE	state-owned enterprise
TNC	transnational corporation
UDHR	Universal Declaration of Human Rights
UNGA	United Nations General Assembly
WB	World Bank
WSF	World Social Forum
WTO	World Trade Organization

HUMAN RIGHTS AND GLOBALIZATION

One day in December 2007, I stood in my local drugstore contemplating which seasonal greeting cards I should buy. Several packages imported from the United States offered twelve cards for Can$14.99. One package imported from China offered twenty cards for Can$5.99. I debated over whether to buy the Chinese cards: Were the workers who produced them exploited? Should I boycott Chinese products? But in the end, I bought them.

This personal debate illustrates the questions about globalization asked by private citizens in the Western world who value human rights. Many wonder whether globalization further impoverishes the underprivileged in poor countries or improves the prospect of their enjoying their human rights, especially economic human rights. Since the early 1990s, there has been much academic discussion about whether globalization is "good" or "bad." Some scholars, notably legal scholars and political scientists, think it obvious that globalization is detrimental to human rights. Schwab and Pollis, for example, focus only on the negative aspects of globalization, stating, "Clearly globalization has had a deleterious effect on the entire complex of human rights" (2000, 217). Other scholars, economists in particular, argue implicitly that globalization can and often does have beneficial effects on human rights (Bhagwati 2004; Legrain 2002).

A core aspect of this debate is whether globalization deepens or relieves poverty. If more people are poor, they are less likely to enjoy their economic human rights; if fewer people are poor, they are more likely to enjoy their economic human rights. However, although the level of poverty does roughly correlate with the likelihood of enjoying economic human rights, it is not the whole story. Whether citizens enjoy their economic human rights is also affected by whether they enjoy their civil and political rights. Moreover, even in societies where civil and political rights are protected, different types of political regimes are more or less likely to protect economic human rights. The type of political regime that exists is in turn influenced by the intensity and objectives of citizens' social movements in defense of human rights. In this book, I argue for the interrelation of all types of human rights and the need for social democracies that will protect them.

The rapidity of globalization causes so much social change in so many parts of the world that it affects billions of people, some to their benefit but many to their detriment. In this situation, the arguments against globalization by popular intellectuals like Naomi Klein (2000) as well as social movement and political leaders are persuasive. They are often easier to follow than the complex arguments of economists, which are very difficult not only for ordinary citizens but also for scholars in other fields to understand. To many critics, contemporary free trade policy—a defining characteristic of globalization—is an unmitigated disaster for the poor, yet some economists argue that it is the best possible solution to poverty. Indeed, the distinguished economist Paul Collier notes his frustration with the "citizens of the rich world, who must take responsibility for their own ignorance about trade policy" (2007, 157).

My purpose in this book is to sort out some of the arguments about the effects of globalization on human rights. Although I respect the international law of human rights and the scholars who refer to it when opposing globalization, I also present some of the economic arguments for globalization. Human rights scholars have a special responsibility to take economics seriously rather than avoid its intellectual challenges. The standards of economic human rights in international law are the standards of the wealthy, industrialized world, of countries that have already experienced economic growth. Human rights scholars must, therefore, understand what creates economic growth, and in order to do so they must try to understand economic analysis, whatever their home disciplines (mine is political sociology). There are no simple ways to predict globalization's probable effects on human rights; its effects vary in different parts of the globe and on different sectors among each country's residents. Those who are interested in human rights need to watch and comment on globalization's effects without resorting to rhetorical objections to or defenses of globalization.

I view globalization as the "second great transformation," referring to Karl Polanyi's classic work, *The Great Transformation* (1944). Polanyi analyzed the great transformation of Britain and Europe from agricultural to industrial societies from about 1780 to 1940; I argue that the contemporary period of globalization involves the transformation of the entire world from agricultural to industrial societies. In chapter 3, I refer to Polanyi while discussing how neoliberal capitalism has transformed the world. In chapters 4 and 5, I investigate two possible theoretical outcomes of globalization's transformation of the world, one positive for human rights and one negative. In chapters 6 and 7, I argue that the second great transformation has the advantage of being characterized by "human rights leapfrogging." The concept and law of human rights, I maintain, has leaped over centuries and oceans to enhance the entire world's capacity to confront the negative aspects of industrialization. Chapter 6 discusses global human rights governance and chapter 7 the global human rights social movement. Chapter 8 explores the possibility of a backward human rights leap caused by the politics of resentment against "Western" globalization and human rights, just as, according to Polanyi, there was a reaction against industrialism in early twentieth-century Europe. Chapter 9 concludes that only social democratic countries can fulfill all aspects of their citizens' human rights but also warns of the various aspects of human insecurity that are exacerbated by globalization.

INTERNATIONAL HUMAN RIGHTS DEFINED

This book refers to human rights as they are defined by international law (Weissbrodt and de la Vega 2007). They are rights to which all human beings are entitled merely by virtue of being biologically human; they are individual rights not tied to group, communal, national, or any other membership. Human rights do not have to be earned, nor are they dependent on any particular social status, such as whether one is male or female. Duty-bearers—those who have duties to protect, promote, and fulfill human rights—are primarily states, although increasingly duties are also imposed on international organizations (IOs) and transnational corporations (TNCs).

The promotion of human rights is one of the principal purposes of the 1945 Charter of the United Nations. The UN's purposes as described in chapter 1, article 1 include "to achieve international co-operation in . . . promoting and encouraging respect for human rights and for fundamental freedoms for all without distinction as to race, sex, language, or religion" (Brownlie and Goodwin-Gill 2006, 4). Human rights are further enshrined in the UN's International Bill of Rights, which consists of the 1948 Universal Declaration of Human Rights (UDHR), the 1966 International Covenant on Civil and Political Rights (ICCPR), and the 1966 International Covenant on Economic, Social, and Cultural Rights (ICESCR) (Brownlie and Goodwin-Gill 2006, 23–28, 348–74).

Civil and political rights include, for example, protection against torture, the right to a fair trial, the right to vote, and the right to act politically through freedom of speech, press, assembly, and association. Economic, social, and cultural rights include the right to work, the right to form trade unions, and the rights to education, social security, an adequate standard of living, and the highest attainable standard of health. So-called collective rights encompass the rights to peace, development, and a clean environment. Civil and political rights are often referred to as first generation rights; economic, social, and cultural rights as second generation; and collective rights as third generation. These generations roughly reflect the chronological development of the international conception of human rights. For the sake of brevity, throughout this manuscript I will refer to economic, social, and cultural rights merely as economic human rights or economic rights, as there is no clear distinction between what is economic and what is social; for example, the right to education could be considered both economic (resulting in higher earning power if one is educated) and social (helping one to participate in the society at large).

Discussion of globalization's effects on human rights tends to focus on economic rights, as critics of globalization are chiefly concerned with its detrimental effects on the poor in developing countries. States have three obligations regarding economic rights: to respect, protect, and fulfill them (Eide 2006, 175). To respect economic rights means not to subvert individuals' enjoyment of them or individuals' capacities to provide for themselves. To protect economic rights means to protect citizens against state and nonstate entities—the latter referring especially to IOs and TNCs—that could undermine their rights. The state's obligation to fulfill economic human rights is the most difficult, as it requires positive intervention in economic, social, and political relations to ensure that citizens enjoy the substance of their rights—that is, that they enjoy their rights not only in principle or in law but also in practice.

Many critics argue that globalization seriously undermines economic human rights by increasing poverty and economic inequality. Chapter 2 investigates these arguments. Globalization has increased inequality within many states and among states; however, the argument that globalization impoverishes more people than it benefits is contentious, as there is much evidence that globalization has significantly reduced poverty worldwide. In any case, alleviation of poverty is often as much a matter of politics, particularly giving the poor a voice and a vote, as it is of economic policy. Therefore, it is important to consider globalization's effects on the political process as well as on economic policy. Critics of globalization do not devote much attention to civil and political rights; indeed, some think of them as a Western phenomenon that should not be imposed on non-Western societies (Thomas 1998, 183). Yet one important aspect of globalization is the worldwide spread of the ideals of democracy, the rule of law, civic equality, minority rights, and individual human rights. Furthermore, despite globalization, states are still sovereign entities. Democratic states that respect the rule of law and protect their citizens' civil and political rights are better able to withstand the detrimental aspects of globalization than nondemocratic states.

The ideals of international human rights are also increasingly incorporated into institutions of global governance such as international financial institutions (IFIs), especially the International Monetary Fund (IMF) and the World Bank (WB), and into the governance structures of some TNCs. This recent trend to require that nonstate actors accept human rights obligations largely results from the actions of human rights nongovernmental organizations (NGOs) and social movements, including the global social movement against, or favoring serious reform of, globalization. However, the creation of new human rights duty-bearers is very recent and far from complete. We cannot yet predict the outcome of the very weak current obligations of IFIs and TNCs for the human rights of the billions of individuals affected by globalization.

It would be easy and satisfying to predict that, in the long run, the international law of human rights will control economic globalization so that its overall effects will be beneficial. But such a prediction cannot be made at this juncture. Equally, however, one cannot positively predict that the overall effects of economic globalization will be harmful to human rights. In this book, I discuss possible intersections of economic change, political change, and social action to demonstrate that politics and social action are the crucial activities that will determine whether globalization undermines or promotes human rights.

GLOBALIZATION DEFINED

Some definitions of globalization focus only on its economic aspects. Bhagwati states, "Economic globalization constitutes integration of national economies into the international economy through trade, direct foreign investment (by corporations and multinationals), short-term capital flows, international flows of workers and humanity generally, and flows of technology" (2004, 3). Other definitions are broader, encompassing social and political as well as economic relations. Held, McGrew, and their colleagues define globalization as "a process (or set of processes) that embodies a transformation in the spatial organization of social relations and transactions, generating transcontinental or interregional flows and networks of activity, interaction, and power" (Held et al. 1999, 483). In a globalized world, everyone lives in "overlapping communities of fate" in which "the very nature of everyday living—of work and money and beliefs, as well as of trade, communications and finance . . . connects us all in multiple ways with increasing intensity" (Held et al. 2005, 1–2).

Space and time are compressed in the new globalized world; the present era is, in effect, the "end of geography" (Bauman 1998, 12). The information revolution began in the 1980s with the widespread use of personal computers and the invention of electronic mail and the Internet. The technology of information transfer, combined with the end of the division of the world economy into socialist and capitalist blocs, facilitated much easier movement of capital across national borders. The constraints of geography also receded as people traveled much more frequently and easily during the late twentieth century. Communication and travel resulted in new global social and cultural arrangements as well as new economic arrangements. The information explosion, the worldwide reach of mass media, and ease of communication affected all cultures. Similarly, ease of travel, migration, and circulation among ancestral and new homes changed social arrangements.

Although globalization includes political, social, and cultural aspects, the chief impetus and beneficiary of globalization is capitalism. I define capitalism as a particular type of market economy in which the costs of labor and of financial and physical capital, in addition to costs like transportation, determine choice of products to be made, the geographical location of production, and the number and types of workers to be employed. Capitalism is the economic system behind new technologies of information and communication and behind the capacity of TNCs to spread worldwide. The technology of information transfer also facilitates much larger and faster finance capital transfers than previously possible. George Soros, the international financier and philanthropist, makes this point in his own definition of globalization as "the development of global financial markets, the growth of transnational corporations, and their increasing domination over national economies" (2002, 1).

For some commentators, capitalism is an evil word, connoting privilege and power for the few over the interests of the many; for example,

O'Connell defines globalization as "a consciously undertaken political project to privilege economic power over public power, in the interests of global and local economic elites" (2007, 492). I agree that unregulated capitalism privileges the rich over the poor; the history of the struggle for human rights in the capitalist Western world is largely a history of workers' struggles for political freedom and economic security. O'Connell, however, refers specifically to the neoliberal economic aspects of globalization, which I discuss in chapter 3. My use of the term "globalization" is broader. I define globalization as a process by which local states, economies, cultures, and social actors are increasingly drawn into a global polity, economy, culture, and civil society. Thus, I refer to the following as aspects of globalization:

- The expanding world market, and international trade and capital flows
- Transnational corporations
- Institutions of global governance, including the international law of human rights, IFIs, and IOs established to regulate the market
- Travel, migration, communication, and global culture
- Global civil society, including international NGOs, global social movements, and other private social actors

Before commencing my discussion of how globalization affects human rights, however, it is necessary to clarify three of its other aspects.

DATING GLOBALIZATION

This book discusses the most recent stage of globalization, which began in the mid-twentieth century and has intensified in the last two decades. There have been earlier episodes of partial "globalization," such as the creation of the Roman and British empires and the opening up of European trade with China. I do not address the debate about the appropriateness of referring to the current round of globalization as a new phenomenon in world history (McNeill 2008). It is enough to note that it is truly global and all-encompassing in its effects.

While there is no consensus on the exact moment at which the world entered this latest round of globalization, the end of World War II may be considered a good starting point. The UN, the first even partially effective institution of global governance, was formed in 1945 as a successor to the League of Nations. The League had been established after World War I to prevent further wars but had failed to avert World War II (MacMillan 2003, 84–86). Before disbanding in 1946, it transferred all its assets to the UN (United Nations Office at Geneva 2008). The League's central mandate became the central mandate of the UN: chapter 1, article 1 of the UN Charter states that one of its central purposes is "to maintain international peace and security" (Brownlie and Goodwin-Gill 2006, 4). The UN quickly expanded to embrace many other goals, including the promotion of human rights. Its member states wrote and endorsed human rights documents, and various UN organs were created both to encourage states to protect human rights and to monitor their progress in doing so (Mertus 2005). The UN also established many subsidiary institutions that helped to ensure that people enjoyed their economic human rights; these include the United Nations Development Program (UNDP), the World Food Program (WFP), and the World Health Organization (WHO).

The founding of the UN coincided with the creation of the Bretton Woods Institutions. At a conference in Bretton Woods, New Hampshire, in 1944, delegates from forty-four nations met to devise new rules for the post–World War II international monetary system. This resulted in the formation of the IMF and the International Bank for Reconstruction and Development, later known as the WB. They were to regulate the international economy to prevent another economic depression like the one that had occurred in the 1930s. The then-prevailing economic orthodoxy was that open markets and free international trade were less likely to cause an international depression than closed markets and restricted trade. The Bretton Woods Institutions evolved in part from the Atlantic Charter, a statement issued by President Franklin Delano Roosevelt of the United States and Prime Minister Winston Churchill of the United Kingdom in 1941. The Charter's aims included not only international economic collaboration but also improved labor standards and social security for all (U.S. Department of State 2008).

The logic behind the creation of the Bretton Woods Institutions in 1944 was the same as the IFI logic promoting world free trade as of the 1980s. From the 1950s to the 1980s, many countries in the "developing" world (as it was then known), especially in Latin America and Africa, experimented relatively unsuccessfully with closed or socialist economies. To remedy these states' perceived failures, the IFIs insisted on open markets and free international trade. They argued that closed markets raise the prices of goods for consumers, who are not able to buy foreign-produced goods that may be cheaper than locally produced ones. Closed markets also permit inefficient production by local producers, who do not need to worry about foreign competition. Thus, closed markets discourage local producers from specializing in those goods for which they have a productive comparative advantage in the international market. This impedes technical and organizational innovation and drives up the cost of goods to consumers worldwide. The Bretton Woods policy of world free trade, still dominant in the early twenty-first century, has caused much economic, political, and social change and inspired much hostility. Critics often identify free trade as promoted by IFIs as the central and most harmful aspect of globalization. Seemingly, the IFIs have forgotten the original mandate of the Atlantic Charter, with its focus on labor standards and social security as well as free trade.

Several other key events define the current round of globalization. In 1978 China moved from economic isolation to active participation in the world economy, experiencing extraordinarily high internal economic growth rates as it became extremely competitive in the global market. In 1989 the destruction of the Berlin Wall, which had previously separated East and West Germany, respectively communist and democratic countries, signaled the end of Eastern European communism. In 1991 the communist regime fell in Russia (formerly the Soviet Union). The formerly closed economies of the communist states were then integrated into international markets. Thus, by the last decade of the twentieth century, there was an almost universal international market economy regulated by an almost universal system of global economic governance.

TIME FRAMES

Predictions about the effects of globalization on human rights depend in part on the time frame used. The first great transformation of Britain and Europe from agricultural to industrial societies took at least one hundred sixty years, from approximately 1780 to 1940 (Polanyi 1944). The second great transformation of the entire world from agricultural and/or socialist economies to capitalist industrial economies will probably take a shorter time, perhaps from twenty to fifty years. This time frame, however, is much longer than that sometimes used to measure effects of globalization.

In 1996 and 1999, *Human Rights Quarterly* published a debate about the relationship between globalization and human rights. The relevant factors in this debate were foreign investment by TNCs (representing globalization) and civil and political rights (representing human rights). William H. Meyer (1996) investigated two contrasting theses. The first was that transnational investment is an "engine of development": TNCs promote economic rights through investment and job creation and promote civil and political rights through the creation of a stable and tolerant political environment. The second was that TNCs undermine national development and by extrapolation undermine improvements in human rights that might result from national development.

Meyer used quantitative data about fifty-two countries in 1985 and twenty-nine countries in 1990 to investigate the relationship between TNC investment and human rights, assuming "a time lag of roughly two to three years between the determinants and the level of human rights" (1996, 390). He compared levels of direct U.S. foreign investment and foreign aid to levels of civil liberties and political rights in recipient countries, as ranked by Freedom House, an American organization that measures political freedom around the world. He also compared the levels of U.S. investment to recipient countries' physical quality of life index (PQLI), an index that combines the infant mortality rate, life expectancy at age one, and adult illiteracy rates. The PQLI is often used as a proxy measure for citizens' enjoyment of their economic rights. Over this very short time period from 1985 to 1990, Meyer found that "the presence of multinational corporations . . . [was] *positively* associated with political rights and civil liberties as well as with economic and social rights in the third world," confirming the thesis that multinational investment was an engine of development (1996, 368; emphasis in the original).

Meyer's conclusion was challenged by Jackie Smith, who with her co-researchers reanalyzed his data, comparing it with her own independent study. Smith used data on civil and political rights from Amnesty International (AI), a major human rights NGO, and the annual reports on human rights produced by the U.S. State Department, as well as WB data on direct foreign investment from all countries, not only the United States. She concluded that there was "little relationship between DFI [direct foreign investment] and political and civil rights practices. . . . The factors that seem to have a much stronger and consistent impact on a government's human rights practices relate to more general structural factors, namely GNP [gross national product] per capita and levels of public debt" (Smith, Bolyard, and Ippolito 1999, 218). Smith's finding that the more general structural factors of GNP per capita and levels of public debt had a stronger impact on a country's human rights performance than TNC investment is directly relevant to the debate on globalization. If globalization stimulates growth in a country's GNP and if, as a result, the country can pay down its national debt, then it will have more resources for provision of economic human rights—assuming a government committed to its citizens' needs.

In the debate just summarized, Meyer and Smith both relied on the assumption that the relationship between globalization and human rights can be measured by data spanning only a few years. I argue that the relationship cannot be predicted over such a short period. Looking to the medium term, a period of about twenty to fifty years, is a more reliable way to ascertain the possible effects of globalization on human rights. This longer time frame permits the scholar to better analyze the social, political, and economic changes that globalization has caused. The most important long-term changes are the adoption of market economies and political democracy. South Korea is a model of almost complete transition from a poor peasant to a wealthy urban society, from a dictatorship to a democracy, over a period of fifty years (Donnelly 1989, 170–78).

China has experienced a very rapid transition from a collectivist command economy to an individualist market economy within thirty years,
yet with a party-bureaucratic dictatorship still in place rather than political democracy. In Eastern Europe and the former Soviet Union, there are
multiple examples of greater and lesser success since 1989 in integrating into the world capitalist system and adopting democracy. Some of the
more economically successful postcommunist countries, such as Hun-
gary, the Czech Republic, and Poland, already show evidence of positive
medium-term change.

One might argue that it is fruitless to look to either the short or
medium term to ascertain the relationship between globalization and
human rights. The eventual outcome of the Industrial Revolution certainly could not have been predicted in Europe in 1780; so, too, the final
outcome of globalization cannot be predicted in the early twenty-first
century. Such an argument, however, would not take into account globalization's capacity to speed up the world. Economic policies change
quickly with international institutions like the IMF and the WB to guide
the changes and with foreign consultants available to teach the rules and
practices of capitalism to willing policymakers and entrepreneurs. For
example, the disastrous "shock treatment" transformation of the Soviet
Union from communism to Mafia-style capitalism resulted from the
advice of IFIs and independent consultants (Stiglitz 2002, 133–65). Similarly, constitutional and legal consultants guide political changes. Social
changes are influenced by transnational NGOs and social movements
that strive to protect and promote human rights while political and economic forces simultaneously undermine them.

Thus, the rest of the world may not need to wait 150 or 200 years before
it is in the same fortunate position as the West was at the end of the Industrial Revolution, enjoying a relatively rights-protective society. Medium-
term analysis does seem possible. Even so, assuming that globalization
will necessarily enhance human rights is unwise. In most societies entering the world capitalist economy, there is severe social disruption. Social
relations in the new global society are more fluid than people in many
parts of the world are used to. Some people are confused by these changes
and long for a simpler time with a stricter normative order; some fight

viciously to retain the old order from which they are being so abruptly torn. In this situation of flux, there is not necessarily a positive correlation between the processes of globalization and the entrenchment of human rights; multiple economic policies, political and legal changes, and social actors affect the final outcome. In each case, moreover, the domestic, national context is as important as transnational, global influences.

NATIONAL SOVEREIGNTY AND DEMOCRACY

Some critics blame globalization for all the adverse conditions for human rights that coincide with it. Many decisions that affect citizens' human rights, however, are made by sovereign national governments. Sovereignty refers to states' legal capacity to make and enforce independent decisions about almost any aspect of their citizens' lives occurring within their borders. Some commentators argue that in the era of globalization states have modified their sovereignty, citing the increasing number of international treaties that states sign and their willingness to submit to international oversight of their adherence to these treaties. For example, the dispute settlement mechanism of the World Trade Organization (WTO) undermines states' economic independence, while the decisions of the UN's Human Rights Committee undermine their political independence. Moreover, some argue, substantive sovereignty has been significantly eroded as states conform to the dictates of IOs and TNCs (Evans 2001, 82). Realizing this, "individuals increasingly seek solutions to their problems outside its [the state's] confines" (Albrow 1997, 73).

Despite the modification of sovereignty that occurs when states sign international treaties, they do retain substantive control over most of what occurs within their territories. There are no international treaties that effectively prevent states from perpetrating severe human rights violations against their own populations; even the 1948 Convention on the Prevention and Punishment of the Crime of Genocide does not require any outside intervention when a state systematically murders its citizens (Brownlie and Goodwin-Gill 2006, 284–87). Only recently has the international community begun to consider its responsibility to protect individuals from these severe violations (Secretary-General 2005; International Commission on Intervention and State Sovereignty 2001). For now, states continue to make their own decisions about whether to protect, promote, and fulfill human rights.

In this respect, the fear that globalization undermines the autonomous decision-making powers of sovereign states seems to idealize the nation state. While "nation-states remain for the foreseeable future the necessary instruments for the provision of security and welfare for their citizens" (Beetham 1998, 65), nondemocratic states are governed by elites who act in their own interests, whether their powers derive from local or global political and economic relations. Such elites are no more likely to protect their citizens' interests against foreign than against local exploiters. Citizens need the democratic right to guide their governments' policies and to change their governments when they so desire, to ensure that their rights are protected.

Political democracy is a necessary, although not sufficient, condition for human rights and their protection (Donnelly 1999; Freeman 2000). Democratic rights can be confined to only a segment of a nation's population, as in the all-white "democracy" of South Africa during apartheid, from 1948 to 1994. In the worst cases, the democratic tyranny of the majority can contribute to civil war as minority groups that feel themselves excluded from power resort to violence. Democracy, then, must be buttressed by the rule of law, political freedoms, and a civic culture of activism if it is to protect human rights, and under these conditions it is more likely than any other type of political system to do so. Rule of law means that the government and its individual members are subject to the same law as ordinary citizens and that judges are independent of political influence. A civic culture of activism and political freedom both precedes and is a consequence of democracy and the rule of law. In most countries, citizens have to fight for freedom of speech, press, assembly, and association, as well as for the vote; indeed, these were some of the earliest human rights campaigns in the Western world (Ishay 2004, 117–72). These rights, once attained, become instrumental in the fight for other rights, especially in establishing welfare states that provide at least minimal guarantees of economic human rights.

Democratic principles of government, the rule of law, and a civic culture of activism took centuries to emerge in the Western world, with intervening episodes of dictatorship and fascism in Europe, severe racism in North America, and systematic discrimination against women and other groups. What are now known as human rights were denied to the vast majority of the West's citizens until well into the twentieth century. Rights-based democratic societies certainly did not emerge through some easy, predictable, and inevitable coincidence of capitalism and human rights. Social actors fought for rights; governments and capitalists capitulated when the costs of not doing so became higher for them than the benefits of repression. These same characteristics of democracy, rule of law, and a civic culture of activism and political freedom must emerge elsewhere if human rights are to be protected. Globalization's various aspects can either impede or promote their emergence, depending on each country's approach both to integration into the world capitalist economy and to political democracy.

Similar to political democracy, economic growth is a necessary condition for economic human rights; in this economists who defend the necessity for economic growth are correct. Economic growth is not a sufficient condition for economic human rights, however. It appears that there are two paths to economic growth, both requiring a market economy. One is the authoritarian capitalist model, as found in East Asia in the mid- to late twentieth century and in China today. The other is the democratic capitalist model, as found in the West in the late nineteenth and twentieth centuries and in countries such as India today. Human rights advocates obviously prefer the latter path, which protects civil and political rights at the same time as economic growth makes protection and fulfillment of economic rights easier. Yet even democratic capitalism does not automatically protect the economic rights of the poor; that requires a social democracy that pays equal attention to civil/political and economic, social, and cultural rights.

A PERSONAL STATEMENT

At this point, I wish to clarify my personal position on the human rights abuses caused by globalization. Every effort ought to be made to ensure that during the process of globalization everyone enjoys her or his full range of human rights, including economic rights. I would like to see a world in which every policy change intended to promote globalization adheres to the principle that the poorest not be rendered even worse off. Thus, I agree with Rawls that "it is not just [fair] that some should have less in order that others may prosper" (1999, 46). Nor do I believe that present generations should suffer abuse of their human rights so that future generations may enjoy them. As Sen argues, "In the context of economic disparities, the appropriate response has to include concerted efforts to make the form of globalization less destructive of employment and traditional livelihood, and to achieve gradual transition" (1999, 240).

My analysis is a theoretical discussion of the possible long-term human rights outcome of globalization; I do not suggest that legal activists, members of civil society, and others who point out its detrimental human rights consequences in the short term should cease their activities. On the other hand, my analysis is meant to persuade readers that in the long run globalization may help to create a world of increased prosperity, democracy, and protection of human rights. This depends, however, on successful social action in defense of human rights. A positive human rights outcome is not inevitable; it is a matter of social action and political decision making.

2

GLOBALIZATION, POVERTY, AND INEQUALITY

Before presenting my argument about the relationship between human rights and globalization, I want to debunk an assumption sometimes found in human rights literature and among some activists critical of globalization: namely, that globalization has caused an increase in world poverty. Thomas, for example, argued in the late 1990s that two-thirds of the world's population had gained little or nothing from economic growth (1998, 165). Ishay argues that intensified global competition has brought "increased poverty to much of the developing world" (2004, 294). Critics also assume that globalization exacerbates inequality both within and among countries, in turn increasing the rate of poverty. Ishay refers to the disturbing trend of a "growing gap between rich and poor countries" (2004, 246), while Falk refers to "accentuating inequities between rich and poor throughout the world" (2006, 121) and Monshipouri, Welch, and Kennedy to "the simultaneous surge in economic growth and inequality" (2003, 965). Thus, many scholars stress globalization's "negative and disabling" effects on human rights rather than its possible beneficial effects (Arat 2006, 19).

These assumptions are so central to the debate about the relationship between globalization and human rights that they require a full discussion of how inequality and poverty are measured and what the results of such measurements are. There is much confusion in the human rights literature between rates of inequality and absolute poverty levels, as measured either by household or individual consumption or income (as discussed in the following pages). Yet absolute poverty is a better proxy measure for any individual's likelihood of not enjoying economic human rights than where she or he falls in world or national inequality rankings. Individual consumption or income level indicates one's absolute level of poverty, regardless of how much others may consume or how much income others may have. It is possible for the rate of absolute poverty to decline even as inequality widens. Thus, even if globalization increases inequality among countries or within a country, it can still raise the absolute incomes of the poorest countries or individuals—an important fact sometimes overlooked by human rights scholars. The international law of economic human rights does not specify that inequalities between the more and less wealthy should be removed; it specifies that every individual should enjoy economic human rights. If the absolute income of the poorest rises with globalization, the poor may be better able to enjoy their economic rights.

Individual inequality within some countries has widened during the last thirty years, but inequality among countries is far less severe than in the centuries and decades preceding globalization. Furthermore, there is no evidence that absolute poverty has increased; indeed, most studies show significant decreases in absolute poverty.

MEASURING INEQUALITY AND POVERTY

Poverty and inequality have different causes, and their effects on human rights can also be quite different. The rate of poverty is usually defined as the percentage of households or individuals living below a certain income; this is called the poverty line. World poverty lines are usually measured at somewhere between $1 and $3 per person per day. Individual inequality rates usually compare the poverty or income levels of percentages of the world's or a country's population—for example, by comparing the income of the top and bottom fifths (quintiles) or tenths (deciles) of the population.

To compare poverty rates with a common poverty line across countries, incomes are typically converted to a common currency using purchasing power parity (PPP) exchange rates rather than market exchange rates (generally measured in US dollars). PPP is calculated by comparing the costs of equivalent "baskets" of goods such as housing, food, and clothing among various countries. Generally speaking, poor countries' per capita PPP figures are higher than their gross domestic product (GDP) or gross national income (GNI) per capita dollar figures, as prices for equivalent baskets of goods are generally lower in poor than in rich countries. For example, China's GNI per capita in 2007 was estimated at $2,360, but its per capita PPP was 5,370, or almost 2.3 times the GNI figure (World Bank 2008a).

World inequality is usually measured using a statistic known as the Gini coefficient, a number ranging between zero and one; the higher the Gini coefficient, the higher the level of inequality. A Gini coefficient of zero means that there is perfect equality (no one has a higher income than anyone else), while a Gini coefficient of one means that one individual possesses all the income. The debate regarding globalization's effect on world inequality revolves around rates of increase or decrease in the global Gini coefficient, which in the period of globalization has usually been in the 0.6 to 0.7 range, depending on what is being measured. Measures of inequality are relative: if everyone's income increases or decreases in the same proportion, measured inequality will not change. But if everyone's income increases, absolute poverty measures will show a decline in the poverty rate. Thus, although inequality and poverty are linked, an increase in inequality is not always associated with an increase in poverty.

As Milanovic explains, there are three different ways to measure international inequality. The first is by comparing the average national income of different countries—for example, by GDP per capita—without weighting for population. In this type of comparison, a very large country like China and a very small country like Barbados have equal weight. Such unweighted comparison can be useful because countries enjoy relative independence in policymaking; thus, comparisons by country can provide information on which types of policies improve economic human rights (Milanovic 2005).

The second type of measurement weights each country by population, so that China's national income is much more influential than that of Barbados. This measurement provides a truer picture of inequality at the individual level, because each individual has the same weight regardless of the country in which she or he lives. Weighted country inequality presents a much better picture of the number of people in the world at each income level, although it still does not differentiate among individuals within countries, assuming instead that each individual within a given country enjoys the same income.

The third type of measurement is the most effective in ascertaining how many people in the world are poor. It uses estimates of household incomes to determine the number of people within each country living at each level. Household incomes are calculated using several types of sources, among which the most prominent are household consumption surveys and estimates based on national accounts; sometimes both sources are combined. Household consumption surveys ask members of a household how much money they spend on things like food, education, or shelter. National accounts measure the entire economic activity of a nation, including the activities of households, governments, NGOs, and corporations; the accounts then generate a GDP or GNI figure, which can be further divided by population to generate GDP or GNI per capita.

Since 1993 the World Bank (WB), to whose figures most human rights scholars refer, has used only household consumption survey data (Milanovic 2005), while some independent scholars have relied on survey data combined with national account data (Bhalla 2002; Sala-i-Martin 2002, 2005). The measure that is used significantly influences estimates of poverty and inequality. Household consumption surveys tend to underestimate income. Among other problems, individual recall of consumption is often faulty and the rich often downplay their consumption or refuse to participate in surveys (Deaton 2004, 19). Surveys do not capture all nonmarket consumption, particularly owner-occupied housing in underdeveloped countries, although WB surveys do take into account consumption of goods produced by the consumers themselves (Ravallion 2003, 10). Household consumption surveys also assume no savings, but some people — even the poor — do save part of their income

(Deaton 2004, 13). Moreover, and very important from the perspective of economic human rights, household consumption figures do not capture "free" (publicly provided) goods such as schooling and health care (Milanovic 2005, 116).

On the other hand, while national accounts do capture publicly provided goods and services, they include figures for financial services and risk-bearing services (insurance), which are only relevant to richer individuals in poor countries (Deaton 2004, 30–31). This may result in overestimates of improvement in the living standards of the poor and underestimates of the level of poverty. Estimated household consumption income can vary widely from estimates of income derived from national accounts; on average, survey income is calculated at less than 50 percent of national accounts income (Bhalla 2002, 218–23).

WORLD INEQUALITY

With these explanations of how income and inequality are measured, we can investigate some statistics. One way to estimate inequality is to refer to wealth—the total amount of assets individuals possess—rather than income, which reflects only what an individual uses (consumes) or earns each year. Figures on distribution of wealth reveal extreme disparities. In 2000 (basing estimates on PPP) the poorest 10 percent of the world's population possessed only 0.1 percent of the world's wealth, as compared to 71.1 percent possessed by the richest 10 percent, 57 percent possessed by the richest 5 percent, and 31.6 percent possessed by the richest 1 percent. Thus, the top 1 percent of the world's population possessed over three hundred times more wealth than the bottom 10 percent (Davies et al. 2006, table 11a). Also in 2000, sixty-seven high-income countries possessed 55.9 percent of the world's net worth, while sixty-four low-income countries possessed only 11.29 percent (Davies et al. 2006, table 8).

Despite these figures, since about 1980 world individual income inequality has not widened. It did widen drastically from the beginning of Europe's Industrial Revolution around 1820 to its peak in the mid-twentieth century. However, the income share of the world's bottom four deciles (40 percent of the world's population) stopped declining between 1980 and 1992 for the first time since 1820, so there was little difference in world distribution in 2002 as compared to 1950 (Bourguignon and Morrisson 2002, 742).

The common claim among human rights scholars that world inequality has increased during the most recent period of globalization (e.g., Pogge 2002, 3) seems to rely on Milanovic's 2002 study of world individual inequality between 1988 and 1993, in which he used household consumption surveys to generate the distribution of persons by PPP. In a later work, Milanovic found that world individual inequality decreased between 1993 and 1998, the latest years for which he had figures; however, it was still wider in 1998 than in 1988. In 1988 the Gini coefficient was 0.619; in 1993, 0.652; and in 1998, 0.642 (Milanovic 2005, 106–9). Using what he calls a "simple accounting procedure" combining household income and national accounts data, Bhalla contends that world individual inequality between 1950 and 2000 reached its peak in 1973 with a Gini coefficient of 0.693, staying at this level for about a decade, after which inequality started to narrow (2002, 174–75).

Sala-i-Martin calculated world individual inequality using a variety of different indicators, including Gini coefficients, the income ratio of the top to the bottom population quintiles, and the income ratio of the top to the bottom population deciles. Regardless of the measure he used, he found that world individual inequality had declined during the period of globalization, whether comparing 1970 to 2000 or 1979 to 2000, as shown in table 2.1 (Sala-i-Martin 2005).

Possibly more significant than any of these figures, which vary according to data source, is the fact that since about 1980 the Gini coefficient for individual inequality has consistently been in the 0.6 range. It is important, however, not to assume that this measure of individual inequality implies stability in inequality among countries. A relatively stable Gini coefficient for individuals does not mean that all countries stayed at approximately the same rank in distribution of world income for the entire period. Rather, some countries' per capita income rose drastically

Table 2.1   World Income Inequality: Individual Indexes

Type of Index	1970	1979	1990	2000	% Change 1970–2000	% Change 1979–2000
Gini Coefficient	0.653	0.662	0.652	0.637	−2.4	−3.8
Top to Bottom Quintile Ratio	10.319	11.048	9.503	8.220	−22.7	−29.6
Top to Bottom Decile Ratio	28.215	30.544	28.137	25.704	−9.3	−17.3

SOURCE: Table III, "World Income Inequality: Individual Indexes," Sala-i-Martin 2005.

while the per capita income of other countries declined. Income distribution within countries also changed; for example, rural-urban inequality within China and India widened (Milanovic 2005, 113). Within-country measures are as important as international comparisons in considering the effects of globalization on economic human rights. But before considering within-country figures, we must look at the changes in absolute world poverty levels over the last few decades.

WORLD ABSOLUTE POVERTY LEVEL

Starting again with the long historical view, since the beginning of the Industrial Revolution the global poverty rate has significantly declined: one estimate is that from 1820 to 1992 the poverty rate fell from over 90 percent of the world's population to 51.3 percent (Bourguignon and Morrisson 2002, 733). Viewed through another lens, average life expectancy more than doubled, from twenty-six years in 1820 to sixty years by 2002 (Bourguignon and Morrisson 2002, 741). Based on a scale of 0 to 100, the Physical Quality of Life Index (PQLI) over 127 countries improved from an average of 50.1 (weighted by population) in 1960 to 71.7 in 1990 (Morris 1996). Furthermore, there is evidence that the rate of world absolute poverty has decreased since about 1980, as shown in table 2.2. Not only has the rate of poverty declined, so also has the depth

Table 2.2   World Poverty Figures by Region, 1981–2005

Region	% Living Below Poverty Line $1.25/day				% Living Below Poverty Line $2.50/day			
	1981	1990	1999	2005	1981	1990	1999	2005
East Asia & Pacific	77.7	54.7	35.5	16.8	95.4	87.3	71.7	50.7
China	84.0	60.2	35.6	15.9	99.4	91.6	71.7	49.5
Eastern Europe & Central Asia	1.7	2.0	5.1	3.7	15.2	12.0	21.4	12.9
Latin America & Caribbean	11.5	9.8	10.8	8.4	29.2	26.0	28.0	22.1
Middle East & North Africa	7.9	4.3	4.2	3.6	39.0	31.2	30.8	28.4
South Asia	59.4	51.7	44.1	40.3	92.6	90.3	86.7	84.4
India	59.8	51.3	44.8	41.6	92.5	90.2	87.6	85.7
Sub-Saharan Africa	53.7	57.9	58.2	51.2	81.0	82.5	83.8	80.5
Total	51.8	41.6	33.7	25.2	74.6	70.4	65.9	56.6

SOURCE: Table 7, Chen and Ravallion 2008.

of poverty; the people who live below the poverty line are not as far below that line as they used to be (Chen and Ravallion 2008, 24).

When calculating poverty rates, scholars take into account inflation and many other factors that might undermine the comparability of the figures they use. Because of population increase, they also refer to percentages of the world's population rather than absolute numbers of the poor. Relying on WB calculations of absolute poverty based on the household survey method, as shown in table 2.2, Chen and Ravallion (2008) used a poverty line of $1.25 per person per day to conclude that between 1981 and 2005 the percentage of the world's population living in poverty decreased from 51.8 to 25.2. This is a decrease in the rate of poverty of more than 50 percent over twenty-four years (calculating the absolute rate of 25.2 percent poverty in 2005 as a percentage of the absolute rate of 51.8 percent in 1981). Using a poverty line of $2.50 per person per day, the decrease was from 74.6 percent of the world's population living in poverty in 1981 to 56.6 percent living in poverty in 2005, or a decline of about 24 percent. These figures can be considered the minimum estimated decline in the rate of absolute poverty, as the WB relies on household consumption surveys, which are more likely to overestimate than underestimate the poverty rate.

Reviewing many surveys of poverty and using a variety of indicators, Bhalla argues that the percentage of the world's population living in poverty significantly declined between 1980 and 2000, regardless of the measure used. Bhalla suggests that a good indicator of world poverty is the percentage of people living on less than $2 per day, which was about 23.3 percent of the world's population in 2000 (2002, 149). Like Bhalla, Sala-i-Martin argues that "the world . . . has had an unambiguous success in the war against poverty rates during the last three decades" (2002, 14). According to his calculations, 5.7 percent of the world's population lived below the $1 poverty line and 10.6 percent below the $2 line in 2000, compared with 15.4 percent below the $1 line and 29.6 percent below the $2 line in 1970. Sala-i-Martin goes even further, calculating a new poverty line of $3 per day, and discovers a decline from 46.6 percent living below it in 1970 to 21.1 percent living below it in 2000 (2005, table 1).

Thus, all the estimates discussed in this section show a downward trend in world poverty levels; claims by some human rights scholars and activists that globalization has increased world poverty are erroneous. On the other hand, poverty has increased and inequality has widened within some countries.

WITHIN-COUNTRY INEQUALITY AND POVERTY

One way to ensure that individuals enjoy economic human rights is to redistribute wealth from the richest to the poorest. Yet, although world poverty levels decreased during globalization, within some countries inequality widened. Among countries, the Gini coefficient ranges from about 0.2 to 0.7; inequality is generally wider in sub-Saharan Africa and Latin America and lower in Asia and the advanced Western industrial democracies. For example, in Canada the Gini coefficient was 0.321 in 2005, in the

United States it was 0.450 in 2007, in Brazil it was 0.567 in 2005, and in Namibia it was 0.707 in 2003 (Central Intelligence Agency 2008).

The benefits of economic growth are less likely to reach the poor in countries with high inequality (Ravallion 2003, 21). High within-country inequality often indicates that the society is organized in such a way that it is difficult for the poorest to participate meaningfully; it may also be an indicator of poor development prospects. With little buying power, the poor are less able to contribute to a country's economic growth, and with poor education and in bad health they are less likely to be employable in growth industries. High within-country inequality may also affect the political process. Demoralized by the contrast between their own living conditions and those of the rich, the poor may withdraw from the political process, rebel, or even turn to crime. Finally, high inequality implies that the poor do not enjoy the human dignity on which all human rights are premised. It suggests that their governments do not take the poorest citizens' needs seriously enough to devote resources to them.

Despite the relevance of within-country inequality, measures of absolute poverty within a country are a better indicator of individuals' enjoyment of their economic rights. A country's integration into the global market can result in both widened internal inequality and higher individual incomes, even for the poorest. To explain theoretically how absolute poverty can be reduced even as within-country inequality widens, I have borrowed data from Bhalla for China, Bangladesh, and Russia in 1980 and 2000 to create table 2.3. Bhalla presents income inequality data in the form of per capita income (PCI) in PPP dollars by quintiles. I compare each country in 1980 and 2000, assuming that in each quintile there is only one individual. I multiply PCI by five and then multiply by the bottom quintile's percent share of national income to find the income of the poorest person in the population of five. I also calculate the absolute change in income for the poorest person and the ratio of the 2000 to 1980 bottom quintile shares and bottom quintile incomes.

As evidenced by table 2.3, widened within-country inequality does not necessarily mean a fall in absolute income for the poorest quintile of the population. The poorest person in China in 2000 received only

Table 2.3   Absolute and Relative Income Compared (national population of 5)

Country	Date	PCI	PCI x 5	% Share of Bottom Quintile	Income Bottom Quintile	Absolute Change in Income	Ratio of 2000 to 1980 (bottom quintile share)	Ratio of 2000 to 1980 (bottom quintile income)
China	1980	907	4535	7.9	358			
	2000	4126	20630	5.9	1217	+859	0.75	3.4
Bangladesh	1980	1102	5510	7.4	408			
	2000	1682	8410	6.2	521	+113	0.84	1.28
Russia	1980	11721	58605	9.5	5567			
	2000	8422	42110	6.7	2821	−2746	0.71	0.51

SOURCE: Calculated from figures presented in table C.1, Bhalla 2002.

75 percent of the share of national income she received in 1980, but her absolute income rose by 859 PPP, so that the ratio of her 2000 to her 1980 income was 3.4:1. In Bangladesh in 2000, the poorest person received only 84 percent of the income share she had received in 1980, but her absolute income rose by 28 percent. In Russia, however, both the income share and the absolute income declined; the poorest person in 2000 received only 71 percent of the share of national income she received in 1980, and her absolute income dropped by 2,746 PPP, so that she received only 51 percent of the income she had received in 1980. This table therefore shows that the income of the poorest can either fall or rise as within-country inequality widens. However, Bhalla's actual numbers are questioned by many other scholars, who argue that he underestimates poverty levels (Milanovic 2005, 127; Ravallion 2003). In the discussion that follows, I rely on poverty estimates by WB scholars, who are less optimistic than Bhalla.

Even if they are correct, the figures in table 2.3 do not reveal anything about a causal relationship between globalization and enjoyment of economic human rights. Although almost all scholars who measure world poverty agree that since 1980 it has been reduced, this does not mean that globalization in and of itself caused that reduction (Ravallion

2003, 3). Indeed, this is the problem with all of the figures discussed in this chapter, whether concerning world or within-country inequality or world or within-country absolute poverty. Globalization, in and of itself, does not increase or decrease the likelihood that individuals will enjoy economic human rights; such enjoyment also depends on preglobalization histories and on government policies affecting human rights both before and during globalization. Often "shifts in [domestic] inequality stem more from domestic education, taxes and social policies" than from globalization (Dollar and Kraay 2002, 121). Even while it is in the process of entering the world economy, a newly globalizing country must pay attention to internal policies. While world redistribution of income depends on many forces not under the control of individual countries, within-country redistribution is a matter that many sovereign states can influence. Historical studies show that as absolute incomes rise, inequality is often mitigated by public policy measures that redistribute income, usually through taxation (Friedman 2005, 351). Thus, it may be that in the future, inequality within the richer "developing" countries will decrease.

POVERTY AND REGIONAL VARIATION

In order to understand how globalization affects poverty, one must also disaggregate world poverty figures. Disaggregation shows that in some regions absolute poverty has been declining since 1980, sometimes quite drastically, whereas in other regions it has increased slightly. Table 2.2 shows world poverty figures per region in 1981, 1990, 1999, and 2005 at the $1.25 and $2.50 per day levels, as calculated by Chen and Ravallion. They caution that these figures do not take into account the adverse effects of fuel and food price hikes since 2005 (Chen and Ravallion 2008, 26), nor do they reflect the effects of the 2008–9 financial crisis.

The greatest reduction in poverty from 1981 to 2005 was in East Asia and the Pacific, including China. This marked reduction resulted from the early growth of the Asian Tiger economies, followed by China's extraordinary growth after 1978. Poverty also fell in South Asia, including India;

like China, India made an autonomous decision to open its internal market to international trade and deregulate its economy. Although not as markedly as in Asia, the poverty rate in the Latin American and Caribbean region also declined. In contrast to the increased prosperity in Asia and Latin America, the poverty rate in Eastern Europe and Central Asia, both parts of the former Soviet Empire, rose in the 1990s but began to decline in the 2000s. The "shock treatment" policy change in the former Soviet Bloc countries from socialized production and provision of basic (even if inadequate) housing and health services to a market economy drove many into poverty, and in retrospect it was considered too fast and too oblivious to the dangers of corruption (Stiglitz 2002, 133–65). By the early twenty-first century, this trend began to reverse itself in some countries, although Russia's prosperity in the 2000s depended heavily on oil revenues (Ahrend 2006, 16). In sub-Saharan Africa, the poverty rate increased between 1981 and 1999 but began to drop in the 2000s as civil wars ended, dictatorships gave way to democracies, and some countries, such as Mozambique, entered the world market economy (Kulipossa 2006).

Regional variation is thus important in considering world inequality. There is no consistent pattern by which the gap between rich and poor countries stays the same or widens. Rather, at different times world inequality is influenced by different factors. Africa's poor economic performance during the 1980s and 1990s lowered the bottom of the international income distribution table; Eastern Europe and Russia's steep decline led to an increase in inequality in the middle of the income distribution. China's and India's prosperity narrowed the disparity between the poor and rich worlds, but inequality between rural and urban China increased world individual inequality again. Meanwhile, the rich world became richer, further widening the gap.

Perhaps more important to the human rights debate, Chen and Ravallion calculated the effects of world income inequality on rates of poverty. They concluded that neither rising inequality between countries nor within countries put a brake on progress in reducing the absolute number of poor in the 1990s. Rather, they said that "the more important factor appears to have been too little growth in average household living standards, given the persistence of the initial inequalities . . . that prevented the poor from participating fully in the growth that did occur" (2001, 299). Thus, economic growth is a necessary, although not sufficient, condition for alleviation of poverty, which is in turn a necessary, although not sufficient, condition for enjoyment of economic human rights. While some human rights scholars and activists focus only on inequality, arguing that reducing inequality is the best means to reduce poverty, many economists instead focus on ways to induce international and national economic growth. Governments, however, must also focus on public policy measures that will permit the poorest to benefit from economic growth.

DO THESE NUMBERS MATTER?

Human rights scholars and activists should be pleased that the rate of poverty decreased dramatically during the late twentieth and early twenty-first centuries. Globalization, Kitching notes, is not a zero-sum game: it is a "sum-sum [positive sum]" game in which various regions of the world can simultaneously be winners (2001, 310). Nevertheless, even if one uses the more optimistic national income figures, 322 million people lived below the WB $1 per day poverty line in 2000; 600 million lived below $2 per day and 1.2 billion below $3 per day (Sala-i-Martin 2005, table 1). According to Chen and Ravallion's 2008 calculations—based on less optimistic household consumption surveys and using $2.50 per day as a benchmark (table 2.2)—the majority of the world's population, 56.6 percent, was still poor in 2005.

The question is, then, what causes an increase or reduction in poverty? What will be the likely effect of globalization on these poor people in the future, and what factors other than globalization will contribute to that effect? It is tempting for those human rights scholars and activists who are severely critical of globalization to attribute all negative changes to globalization and all positive changes to resistance to it. The "pro-poor growth" of countries like China and India suggests that such a perspective lacks a nuanced understanding of global economics, especially the neoliberal economics decried by globalization's critics. Indeed, "the contribution of globalization to inequality, such as it was, came as those countries that did not participate [in globalization] fell behind those that did" (Friedman 2005, 368). Combined with government measures meant to promote both economic and civil/political human rights, globalization can promote enjoyment of economic human rights.

3

GLOBAL NEOLIBERALISM

THE SECOND GREAT TRANSFORMATION

Globalization is the second great transformation—the second time that capitalism has transformed international economic and social relations in much of the world. In *The Great Transformation* (1944), Karl Polanyi explained the economic, social, and political changes that occurred in Europe, particularly Britain, from the last two decades of the eighteenth century to World War II. Those years saw a radical transformation in the way that most people lived. Peasants became artisans and members of the urban working class; they migrated from villages to cities and moved from closed, church-based societies to more open, secular communities. A new class of industrialists arose. Polanyi especially emphasized the newness of a society based primarily on the quest for material gain and the very rapid end of the "social," which had integrated people's productive and personal lives within a dense network of overlapping social ties. Impersonal market relations superseded the personal relations of reciprocity and redistribution that had previously regulated social life, in which family, kin, and village members exchanged favors and informally redistributed wealth. In the new society, individuals in their different roles as family members, producers, and community members increasingly related to one another primarily within the marketplace (Durkheim 1933).

In the feudal society of precapitalist Europe, land had been the basis not only of peasants' economic security but also of their connection to the places and communities of their birth. Landlords and peasants had mutual obligations. In principle, although often not in practice, landlords controlled distribution of land and stored food in anticipation of shortages, thus ensuring peasants' minimum economic security. This was a hierarchical society, though, in which landlords could enforce peasants' obligations much more easily than peasants could enforce those of their landlords.

During the first great transformation, land became a commodity to be used by landlords as they saw fit, even if such use meant expelling the peasants, as in the British enclosure movement. In a "revolution of the rich against the poor" (Polanyi 1944, 35), landlords enclosed properties with fences, driving off the peasants in order to raise sheep to produce wool for the new international (European) market. Peasants migrated to cities where, transformed into industrial workers, they depended on factory owners who had little sense of personal obligation to them (Marx [1867] 1967). The obverse side of industrial poverty and exploitation, however, was individuals' new freedom to escape their inferior social status and seek their own fortunes. This freedom was the precursor to that being experienced by hundreds of millions of individuals now entering the global capitalist economy during the second great transformation.

In the twenty-first century, throughout what were formerly noncapitalist or only partly capitalist societies, the social is giving way to the profit motive, as it did earlier in western Europe. It seems that the social has disappeared and that those with power over ordinary people no longer feel any sense of obligation to them. The transnational corporations (TNCs)—symbols of globalization—seem to feel little obligation to their local employees or suppliers and even less to the local communities in which they invest. TNC investors enjoy "freedom from the duty to contribute to daily life and the perpetuation of the community," demonstrating a "disconnection of power from obligations" (Bauman 1998, 9).

For many individuals, globalization makes economic security dependent on their ability to find scarce, often very poorly paid employment in the marketplace. The protection of belonging to a community, however materially poor it is, gives way to urban anomie—the feeling that no one cares, no one is there to help, no one knows who you are. One's place of origin no longer guarantees communal assistance. A myth is propounded of self-regulating markets as sufficient for economic growth, and growth as sufficient to fulfill citizens' material needs, just as nineteenth-century doctrines of laissez-faire economics replaced public commitment to the social good in newly industrializing Britain (Stiglitz 2001). Billions of people now experience an "avalanche of social dislocation" (Polanyi 1944, 40).

In a sermon in the English city of York in 1014, Archbishop Wulfstan said, "The world is in a rush, and is getting close to its end" (Giddens 2003, 1). This is the reaction of many people to the current era: globalization is a sense of "things getting out of hand" (Bauman 1998, 59). Just as capitalism transformed Britain and Europe, now it is transforming the former global south, areas of the world that as late as the mid-twentieth century were not industrialized. Globalization intensifies the pursuit of private interest and creates a social system in which individuals are increasingly disengaged from family, village, and community. It undermines what is left of purely local institutions. Globalization thus seems to be a process that is out of control, destroying traditional societies, local values, and local economies.

Yet despite these social costs, globalization seems the only path to long-term economic growth for most of the world and thus a necessary condition for the attainment of economic rights. As Sen states, "The one solution [to the problems caused by globalization] that is not available is that of stopping global trade and economies" (1999, 240). Nevertheless, there are many severe short-term costs on the path to sustained economic growth.

DEVELOPMENT AND ECONOMIC HUMAN RIGHTS

Many critics of globalization believe it to be responsible for poverty in the global south, despite the statistics discussed in chapter 2 that show a decrease in poverty during globalization. To Falk, for example, globalization is a "predatory" takeover of the world by neoliberal capitalism.

It is a zero-sum game invented by the world's capitalist nations and international managers for their own benefit, especially in international financial institutions (IFIs). Globalization is not necessarily predatory, however. Falk concedes that it "could have occurred and might still be redirected under a variety of ideational auspices other than neo-liberalism" (1999, 2). If international and domestic markets are regulated and states intervene to protect their citizens' economic human rights, then globalization may have more beneficial than harmful effects.

Globalization seems to impose the capitalist way of life on hitherto traditional societies, yet most traditional societies were changing decades before the latest phase of globalization began, often as a consequence of development plans imposed by their domestic rulers. The idea of development, implying concern for citizens' well-being as opposed to simply economic growth, became fashionable in the early postcolonial period, when the world turned its attention to ways to remedy poverty in newly independent countries. The principle of development improved upon the proposition that all previously traditional societies could simply follow the Western model of economic growth. Most definitions of development in the early postcolonial period referred to some combination of economic growth, national or regional economic self-reliance, and international and national redistribution of wealth. Self-reliance, it was thought, could occur in part through import substitution, an economic policy whereby states encouraged local production of goods and imposed high tariffs on imports that competed with local products. This policy was especially popular and relatively successful in Latin America (Stiglitz 2006, 35–37), but it was not sustainable in the long run, as the domestic market on which protected producers could rely was limited.

Another popular path to development was socialism. Many political leaders in the south thought that they could achieve growth, self-reliance, and redistribution via a state-directed command economy. Seduced by the Soviet model (not yet discredited) and by the Soviet Union's offers of aid to countries that followed its advice, these political leaders honestly believed that they could best help their citizens if they took over the commanding heights of the economy rather than leaving citizens to make their own living as they saw fit. In Africa, the Soviet collectivist model was thought to conform more closely than capitalism to traditional community-based social organization. However, African resistance to market forces proved to be disastrous (Howard 1986).

One cause of the economic disasters in Africa and elsewhere was that some political leaders of newly independent countries had personal motives for favoring centralized control of national economies. State direction of the economy provided enormous opportunities for corruption. To justify such corruption, these leaders defended "developmental dictatorships." Citizens, they argued, did not need civil and political rights when they were starving. The right to food had to be fulfilled before other rights could be considered, and only a command economy could fulfill the right to food. Rulers deflected citizens' attention from their own corruption by attributing their countries' continued poverty to the international trade system rather than to the deficiencies of command economies. Corrupt political leaders blamed the north's neocolonial exploitation of the south for the continued poverty of former colonies.

By the 1970s, it was popular to argue that development required reorganization of the world economic system. In 1974 the United Nations General Assembly (UNGA) declared a New International Economic Order (NIEO) (United Nations General Assembly 1974). A key NIEO theme was international equity, the need for economic fairness between the developed and developing regions. The NIEO proposed that fairness required interference in the international free market—for example, by instituting a "just and equitable relationship" between the prices of exports and imports of developing countries to improve their unsatisfactory terms of trade (United Nations General Assembly 1974, article 4, j). Terms of trade refers to the ratio between the prices of goods a nation exports and the prices of goods it imports. Critics of the world economic system believed that the richer countries underpaid the poorer countries for their products in a system of unequal exchange (Brown 1974, 229–55). Nevertheless, fairness still included "the right of every country to adopt the economic and social system that it deems most appropriate" (United Nations General Assembly 1974, article 4, d). The NIEO called on developed countries to change international prices but did not call on developing countries to remedy inefficient socialist ·or protectionist economic policies or the rampant corruption crippling many nations.

By the 1980s, developmental dictatorships were discredited. The self-interest of political leaders in denying both economic goods and political freedoms to their citizens had become obvious, and the failures of the Soviet model were well known. In 1986 the UNGA proclaimed a new Declaration on the Right to Development, focusing not only on fairness in the international system but also on the interaction of all types of human rights. It defined the right to development as "an inalienable human right by virtue of which every human person and all peoples are entitled to participate in, contribute to, and enjoy economic, social, cultural and political development, in which all human rights and fundamental freedoms can be fully realized" (United Nations General Assembly 1986, article 1, 1). Thus, the declaration acknowledged both that development was a right to which individuals—not states—were entitled and that development depended in part on enjoyment of civil and political rights. Yet it still called for a NIEO (article 3, 3).

The Declaration on the Right to Development had no practical influ-
· ence on the organization of international trade. Moreover, it had little, if any, effect on IFIs, especially the World Bank (WB) and the International Monetary Fund (IMF), which by the 1980s were stressing the classic preoccupation with economic growth over the more nebulous idea of development. According to the IFIs, the self-sufficiency and import substitution models previously tried in Africa and Latin America were economically irrational measures that increased the prices of locally made goods and discouraged local innovation to produce better goods more cheaply. The best path to economic growth was entry into a competitive international market; developing countries should export goods that they could produce cheaply and use the foreign currency they earned to import other goods. The IFIs also advocated transnational investment and encouraged developing economies to reduce or eliminate barriers that might discourage it. This revived perspective on international trade and investment, harkening back to the economic principles of the Bretton Woods Institutions, was dubbed "neoliberal." "Liberal" in this reading meant an economic system in which individuals and corporations

pursued their own economic self-interests unhampered by cumbersome regulations.

Critics denigrated the IFIs' claim that the most efficient path to economic development was through a market economy in which the state did not interfere. The IFIs ignored historical evidence that the state had been actively involved in capitalist development in the Western world. In the nineteenth century, for example, the U.S. government gave land grants to railway companies and financed the first telegraph line, just as it funded the research that resulted in the Internet in the late twentieth century (Stiglitz 2006, 20). There was no completely "free" market in the prosperous Western world; all rich economies had countless regulations and many countries subsidized or protected particular productive sectors.

The IFIs also ignored evidence that economically successful East Asian countries had developed with substantial government participation. In 1957 South Korea was as poor as Ghana (Werlin 1994). South Korea pursued an export-oriented growth policy, concentrating on its comparative advantage in at first producing labor-intensive, cheap consumer products, then moving to more capital-intensive, expensive products such as automobiles and computers. At the same time, however, the South Korean government promoted and protected its import substitution industries. It also invested heavily in education and redistributed Japanese-owned land after World War II, so that the peasantry was not impoverished as the industrial economy grew (Toussaint 2006). Similarly, other East Asian countries prospered via export-led growth but simultaneously invested in social policies to reduce poverty and inequality (Stiglitz 2002, 92). East Asian governments were actively involved in industrialization policy and the move to free trade, and they sometimes used short-term infant industry protection as a means to' promote industrial growth (Jomo 2003, 13).

In the 1980s, then, the IFIs imposed a development model on the world's remaining poor countries that had no historical precedent. The IFIs recommended that still-underdeveloped states renounce import substitution, socialist redistribution, and almost all government interference in the free market, yet neither the Western world nor East Asia had developed solely by reliance on an unfettered free market. As one critic argued, IFIs viewed the world through "neoliberal tinted glasses" (Thomas 1998, 166).

NEOLIBERAL CAPITALISM

Globalization, critics contend, is driven by the ideology of neoliberalism, which privileges corporate profits over the interests of both states and human beings. "Neoliberal globalization . . . entail[s] the reform of both state policies and institutions, typically under the supervision of the international financial institutions, and . . . [reshapes] the rules and practices governing world trade, foreign investment, and financial flows" (Sandbrook et al. 2007, 215). Human rights advocates are especially concerned by three aspects of neoliberal economics: structural adjustment programs (SAPs), free international capital flows, and free trade. There is much evidence that the first two aspects cause more harm than good to developing economies, but the evidence regarding the third is mixed.

During the 1980s and 1990s, IFI loans and grants were frequently conditional on recipient states' adoption of SAPs, which were meant to streamline formerly inefficient economies, reduce state interference in the marketplace, and reduce spending by highly indebted states. Key aspects of SAPs included devaluation of national currencies, introduction of more secure property rights, privatization of state-owned enterprises (SOEs), and reduction in social spending and the size of the civil service. Currency devaluation makes a country's exports more attractive on the international market because they are cheaper relative to other currencies. Securer property rights and sale of SOEs to private buyers are thought to promote productive efficiency. Reduction in state spending and the size of the civil service is meant to release funds to pay off the national debt. The IMF also required borrowing countries to liberalize trade, making exporting and importing easier. All of these policies seem like sound economic measures that will help secure a country's long-term economic growth. However, critics argue that the IFIs' real motive in promoting unhampered market economies is to enable developing countries to repay their debts to the IFIs (Easterly 2006, 227), to developed countries, and to private lenders.

Most SAPs adversely affected economic human rights in the countries that adopted them. SAPs undermined children's right to education by eliminating policies that guaranteed free compulsory primary education and reducing the funds used to support schools and pay teachers (Tomasevski 2006). SAPs may also have undermined the right to food (Kent 2008, 18). Many countries that accepted SAPs sold formerly state-owned industries to private owners, in the process laying off many employees. To save money, governments also laid off many public servants. In some cases, public goods such as water and electricity were privatized, driving up the costs to private consumers and sometimes charging them for what had previously been "free" (publicly provided) goods (Sachs 2005, 275).

In a statistical study of 131 developing countries between 1981 and 2003, Abouharb and Cingranelli found that SAPs had adverse effects on economic rights in all but a few countries. They also negatively affected personal integrity rights such as freedom from torture and workers' rights (2007, 170–202). The political process by which SAPs damaged human rights in most recipient countries could be roughly summarized as "hardship—conflict—repression" (2007, 24). SAPs increased political repression as governments enforced unpopular austerity measures, including reduced food subsidies. Demonstrations against the IMF for imposing SAPs became common; in the first nine months of 2000 alone, demonstrations occurred in six Latin American and four African countries (Easterly 2006, 218).

The detrimental effects of SAPs were not universal: in a few cases, such as Ghana and Uganda, the effects were mixed and perhaps even beneficial for some citizens' economic human rights. However, Ghana and Uganda may have progressed in part because they received more foreign aid as a reward for introducing SAPs (Dicklitch and Howard-Hassmann 2007). In some instances, the adverse effects of SAPs may actually have been caused by the IMF's practice of giving governments money even when they consistently failed to implement the required policies (Easterly 2006, 227). Some governments simply lacked the institutional capacity to properly administer SAPs, even when to do so might have been in the best interests of the national economy. Indeed, governments were occasionally at fault for SAPs' negative consequences: for example, they could have reduced spending on armaments rather than on social welfare (Bhagwati 2004, 89). It was estimated that Sudan spent almost 47 percent of its government budget on the military in the 1990s, as opposed to only 1.7 percent on education (Tomasevski 2006, 10). In other cases, however, the IMF determined the particular budget cuts.

Despite the hardship-conflict-repression nexus, SAPs did coincide with improved democracy (Abouharb and Cingranelli 2007, 203–24). This may have been because by the 1990s the IFIs had begun to promote good governance, recognizing that without financial transparency and accountability to the public, the development projects and economic policies they advocated could easily fail. In a virtuous circle, democracy is positively correlated with economic development and economic rights; all three promote one another. Unfortunately, the negative effects of SAPs on the living standards of hundreds of millions of people may well have cancelled out the democratic benefits of IFI pressures on previously undemocratic states.

The second aspect of neoliberal economics that appears to have had detrimental effects on economic human rights is free international capital flows. Technical changes in information technology—a central aspect of globalization—make it possible for money to be transferred instantaneously; in the early twenty-first century, an estimated $2.5 trillion per day was transferred from one location to another (Brysk 2005, 62). Although a very strong advocate of free trade, Bhagwati warns against the speed with which finance capital can enter or be withdrawn from a country (2004, 199–207). Soros, himself an international financier, also warns against the dangers of uncontrolled financial transfers (2002, 109–15).

"Hot money" is the term often used for these transfers. Stiglitz defines hot money as "money that comes into and out of a country, often overnight, often little more than betting on whether a currency is going to appreciate or depreciate" (2002, 7). He criticizes the IMF for encouraging hot money to enter a country without regard to its government's economic goals. Hot money investors look for quick profits in the financial market, not longer-term profits requiring investment in infrastructure or manufacturing. Often, financiers transfer funds for purely speculative reasons; they buy cheap currency in hopes of selling it when its value rises, but they sell it if they believe its value will fall. Once they start selling, the currency's value falls even more, thus exacerbating the crisis, as the hot money flees the country as quickly as it entered (Kitching 2001, 49–82).

This hot money phenomenon precipitated the Southeast Asian economic meltdown of 1997–98. The growing countries of East Asia had been attractive to international investors, but in 1997 the Thai baht (Thailand's currency) collapsed and currency traders immediately began to move money out of the region. "Excessively rapid financial and capital market liberalization was probably the single most important cause of the crisis" (Stiglitz 2002, 89). Countries that had followed IMF prescriptions for liberalization of financial flows were more vulnerable than countries that had instituted controls on them. Malaysia, which refused to accept uncontrolled investment, did not succumb as severely as other countries to this economic crisis (Stiglitz 2002, 93).

There is a difference, however, between hot money financial transfers and direct foreign investment (DFI). DFI is long-term investment in production by TNCs. Critics commonly protest that domestic governments protect DFI by enforcing laws that undermine workers' rights. Evaluating statistical studies of DFI's effects on domestic political repression, however, Hafner-Burton found "very little evidence to show that FDI [DFI] might increase government repression" (2005, 693). Evidence actually suggests that foreign investment sometimes helps local economies. Often, investors introduce advanced technology (Kitching 2001, 103). They sometimes also improve workers' rights by introducing best practices of management-worker relations, in part because it is organizationally inefficient for the same corporations to have different practices in different countries.

The third aspect of neoliberal capitalism, free trade, does not seem to have had the same detrimental consequences for economic human rights as SAPs and hot money financial transfers. Indeed, the progress made by many countries that have adopted freer trade since the 1970s confirms the original prescriptions of the Bretton Woods Institutions. Defenders of globalization argue that by intensifying a country's involvement in international trade, globalization improves its capacity for economic growth and thus its potential for realization of citizens' economic human rights (Bhagwati 2004; Besley and Burgess 2003). The taxes and other revenues generated by a growing economy provide governments with the resources they need to fulfill economic rights. Moreover, with more opportunities to participate in the global economy, local producers, workers, and peasants find it easier to provide for themselves. Despite all its costs, globalization is the fastest path to long-term economic growth, which is necessary, although not sufficient, for improved economic human rights.

Some statistical studies confirm the positive connection of free trade to human rights. Milner found that "global integration as measured by [trade] regime membership and trade openness has a positive effect on subsistence rights," whereas financial openness had a negative effect on basic human needs (2002, 86). Hafner-Burton's findings were more nuanced: she reported that "high-trading states that are not export-driven are less likely than low-trading states to repress human rights over time, while export-driven economies are . . . more likely to repress." Overall, she concluded that "trade flows may encourage a wide variety of different governments to support better human rights practices" (2005, 691–92). Although Hafner-Burton focused on political repression, not economic human rights, countries that are politically free are more likely to develop economically than countries that are politically unfree (Sen 1999).

Critics of globalization frequently target the World Trade Organization (WTO), which was created in 1995 to facilitate international free trade, particularly by removing trade barriers such as tariffs on imports and by cutting domestic subsidies for goods that might otherwise succumb to competition from imported products. The WTO does not impose its policies on states; rather, states voluntarily join the WTO and decide by consensus which barriers to remove (Jones 2004). Yet in 2008, wealthier parts of the world, notably the United States and the European Union (EU), still subsidized their own agricultural producers and imposed tariffs on goods imported from poorer parts of the world, especially but not only on food. This meant that poor countries were unable to export their goods to rich countries that charged protectionist import tariffs. Nor could farmers in poor countries compete with cheap subsidized foods imported from richer countries. On the other hand, urban consumers in these poor countries benefited from the subsidized food imported from the United States and EU (Sachs 2005, 282; Rodrik 2008). Often, some poor are made worse off as others are made better off; different sectors of the population win or lose as neoliberal economic policies are introduced (Kanbur 2007, 2).

Some countries that entered the free trade regime in the late twentieth century experienced reduced poverty rates. This reduction, however, is most evident in Asia, where states entered the global free market voluntarily, not at the behest of the IMF or as a result of loan conditionality. China and India grew rapidly once they turned to the global market economy—in China's case abjuring collectivized and state-owned enterprise, and in India's case renouncing protectionism. Nevertheless, the Chinese government carefully regulated its new economic policy.

Some critics believe that China is a special case that should not be considered when assessing the effects of globalization. They prefer to exclude China, referring only to the rest of the "underdeveloped" world. Yet Vietnam, a smaller country than China, also experienced high growth after opening up to the world market economy (International Monetary Fund 2006; Wells-Dang 2002), as did many other underdeveloped countries. If China is to be excluded from consideration of globalization's possible economic benefits, then sub-Saharan Africa, the poorest region of the world, should be excluded from consideration of the possible harm globalization causes. Sub-Saharan Africa is also a special case: in wide swathes of central, east, and southern Africa, HIV/AIDS has reduced the growth rate and undermined living standards. Yet following negative growth rates from 1980 to 2000, even sub-Saharan Africa exhibited positive rates in the twenty-first century after some countries ended their civil wars, improved their internal governance, partially controlled corruption, and reformed their economies. In 2006 the rate of growth for sub-Saharan Africa as a whole was about 5.5 percent (International Monetary Fund 2007).

Nonglobalizing countries that do not attract international capitalist investment have weaker economies and lower growth rates than countries that do (Dollar and Kraay 2002, 126). The world's six billion people are divided into three groups: the top billion (the developed Western world and Japan); the middle four billion in growing, globalized economies; and the bottom billion (Collier 2007). Almost three of the middle four billion live in a new group of growing middle-income countries, often known collectively as BRICSAM (Brazil, Russia, India, China, South Africa, and Mexico). These economically rising countries are challenging the former economic and political hegemony of the United States (Khanna 2008). The bottom billion is concentrated in sub-Saharan Africa, former Soviet Central Asia, and a few other countries such as Haiti and Burma. Globalization did not cause the bottom billion's poverty. Rather, the causes are primarily civil wars, lack of access to international shipping routes, heavy reliance on natural resources, and bad governance (Collier 2007).

Thus, by the twenty-first century there was no longer any global south, in economic terms; this rhetorical appellation ignored the separation of the world's former underdeveloped regions into distinct blocs. No matter how often the euphemism of "developing" is applied to the countries in which the bottom billion live, many still have negative growth rates. The challenge with regard to these countries is finding ways for them to profitably join the global economy, not withdraw from it (Collier 2007, 79–96).

REFORMING ECONOMIC GLOBALIZATION

Globalization can promote economic growth, which in turn can reduce poverty, which in turn can help ensure that people enjoy their economic rights, but the type of globalization matters. Poverty reduction does not require that the state cease to regulate the economy; indeed, such a policy appears antithetical to economic growth and economic rights. Domestically induced openness to trade, combined with some protection of domestic industries and markets, seems to be a better path to economic growth than unregulated integration into the international market at the behest of IFIs.

The detrimental effects of IFI policies in the 1980s reinforced international criticism of free market economies. In the 1990s critics began to exert more influence on the IFIs. Integration into the global marketplace, they showed, was not always sufficient to promote growth. In any case, even if the IFIs were correct and integration was indeed the best path to economic growth, growth alone was insufficient to ameliorate poverty. The IFIs reacted to this criticism by requiring countries borrowing from the IMF to write Poverty Reduction Strategy Papers (PRSPs), based in part on civil society input, and to devote some of their funds to remedying poverty. However, critics argued that the IFIs still required PRSPs to adhere to the free trade policies that had earlier characterized SAPs. They also contended that the IFIs simply ignored the civil society recommendations for policies such as import substitution (Mouelhi and Ruckert 2007). Although the IFIs stressed country and civil society "ownership" of PRSPs, local governors and citizens were often pressured into acknowledging ownership of policies with which they actually disagreed (Easterly 2006, 195–99).

The IFIs' decision around 1990 to stress accountability, transparency, and good governance as key aspects of development may have been more effective in protecting economic human rights than the introduction of PRSPs. These policies were less politically sensitive than explicit promotion of civil and political rights, but they did mandate that governments should be accountable to their citizens; that procedures and expenditures should be transparent, not secretive and possibly illegal; and that government should be efficient and based on the rule of law. In short, they introduced some of the basic underpinnings of democratic rule. Democratization helps to ensure that the benefits of growth reach the majority of citizens. The spread of democracy, the rule of law, and civil and political human rights give some of the poor a voice they previously did not have.

Nevertheless, real amelioration of the problems of poverty can only occur with strong political organization. No amount of vigilance by the world human rights community will adequately protect those now being incorporated into the global capitalist system unless domestic political actors are permitted to voice their concerns about globalization. The likelihood that globalization will have a positive effect on economic human rights depends to a large extent on political action from below—by citizens—against states, international organizations (IOs), and corporations. In chapters 4 and 5, I show theoretically how globalization and the internal political, economic, and social changes it induces can either positively or negatively affect promotion and protection of human rights.

A POSITIVE MODEL

THE METHODOLOGY OF IDEAL TYPES

In this chapter and the next, I propose two complex ideal-type models of positive and negative relationships among globalization, economic development, and both civil/political and economic human rights. "Ideal type" is a phrase coined by the early twentieth-century German sociologist Max Weber. Ideal types do not describe any actual existing situations but "[construct] certain elements of reality into a logically precise conception," thus showing the differences between types rather starkly (Gerth and Mills 1958, 59).

The ideal types I present are my own models of two sets of social changes, one induced by transnational investment and the other induced by transnational capital flight. In each case the class structure of society undergoes change as an industrial working class, a professional and entrepreneurial middle class, and a wealthy propertied class are created. The interactions among these three classes sometimes result in the emergence of a new social ideology of liberalism, freedom, and equality, which in turn affects the likelihood that a democratic system of government subject to the rule of law will develop. Social action by civil society groups—groups of private citizens acting on their own behalf or on behalf of others—also influences how these changes in society, ideology, and governance intersect. In other cases, however, the interactions among the three social classes result in exclusionist ideologies and antidemocratic tendencies, both in government and among civil society groups.

Thus, I use ideal types to show how globalization can result in both positive and negative social changes. Following Meyer (1996) and Smith (Smith, Bolyard, and Ippolito 1999), as discussed in chapter 1, I use investment by transnational corporations (TNCs) as a proxy for economic globalization. TNCs are corporations that invest, produce, or sell in at least two countries. Adopting the proxy of TNC investment generates complex models, and there is no suggestion in either model of any necessary relationships, nor are these models complete pictures. However, they do show that the connection between globalization and a rights-protective society is complex and contingent. I base the positive model largely on a retrospective history of the development of western Europe and North America, and the negative model on Stiglitz's description of the 1997 economic meltdown in Asia (2002, 89–132). In the positive model, TNCs engage in actual direct foreign investment (DFI), while in the negative model they engage in get-rich-quick financial transactions of the hot money type described in chapter 3.

Both models refer to the longer term; neither describes the actual effects of globalization on human rights in the short term. Nor do the models refer only to the effects of globalization on poverty or inequality. While poverty and inequality are key measures of whether globalization assists or hinders realization of economic human rights, analysis of legal, social, and political factors is also necessary in order to understand globalization's effects on human rights. This requires speculation about social change and how multiple factors affect one another.

MARKET ECONOMIES AND HUMAN RIGHTS

The international law of economic human rights elaborates the obligations of states to protect and implement those rights, as in the right to food (Kent 2005a). Yet there are real constraints on the resources states command and on human capacities to organize and administer them;

international laws protecting economic human rights cannot, on their own, overcome these constraints. Without a productive economy creating goods that private citizens can buy and sell or governments can redistribute, states cannot guarantee enjoyment of economic rights.

Proponents of globalization often argue that free markets underpin the most productive economic system—by implication the one that best improves economic human rights. They maintain that human material betterment in poor countries depends on economic growth; without such growth, there are not enough material goods to protect citizens' basic welfare. One such proponent is the Indian economist Jagdish Bhagwati. In his youth, he favored India's closed, protectionist, quasi-socialist economy. Gradually, however, he became persuaded that Indians were more likely to prosper if they lived in an open, growth-oriented economy (Bhagwati 2004).

George W. Bush, president of the United States from 2001 to 2009, also advocated the virtues of a free market economy. "Free markets and open trade are the best weapons against poverty, disease, and tyranny," he said (2002, 78). "When nations close their markets and opportunity is hoarded by a privileged few, no amount of development aid is ever enough. But when nations respect their people, open their markets, expand freedom and opportunity to all their citizens, entire societies can be lifted out of poverty and despair" (White House 2004, 2). Bush's statements may seem overly optimistic; nevertheless, the argument for connections between a market economy, economic growth, democracy, and (eventually) human rights must be taken seriously.

Market economies encourage citizens to use their own productive capacities to support themselves. As Sen (1999) argues, citizens must be permitted to exercise their own capabilities. The freedom and opportunity that Bush rhetorically defended are means by which citizens can find ways to make a living. When they rely on their own productive capacities, they can create goods and wealth for their own use or to sell in the marketplace; thus, they can satisfy all or some of their own economic needs without reliance on the redistributive powers of the state. This is one major reason why socialist economies fail: the state denies citizens the right to take advantage of the market opportunities that they identify.

In socialist economies, the state also undermines the right to private property, in some cases abolishing it completely, as in economies that do not even permit citizens to own houses they have built or small businesses they have established. Yet economic growth is best stimulated by efficient creation of and participation in a market economy that protects property rights (Kimenyi 1997, 12–98). The macroeconomic reforms advocated by international financial institutions (IFIs) frequently include entrenchment of legal property rights.

Property rights are often accrued when some social actors evict others from the land they occupy, as in the British enclosure movement or, to use Karl Marx's phrase, in other situations of "primitive accumulation" preceding the actual evolution of capitalist production ([1867] 1967, 713–16). During the nineteenth-century California gold rush, for example, prospectors divided up the land themselves; the government later legalized the procedures they had devised (Easterly 2006, 93). In the process, one can assume, any rights Native Americans might have had by virtue of prior occupancy of the land were ignored. In early post-Soviet Russia, a few individuals who were experienced in wending their way through the black market of socialist times accrued vast wealth when the economy was suddenly opened up to private property; they eventually became the "oligarchs" in a new capitalist system in which tens of millions of others were impoverished (Stiglitz 2002, 133–66; Chua 2004).

Property rights have an ambiguous history as a human right. While they are included in the 1948 Universal Declaration of Human Rights (UDHR), they are not included in the 1966 International Covenant on Civil and Political Rights (ICCPR) or the 1966 International Covenant on Economic, Social, and Cultural Rights (ICESCR). In article 17, the UDHR states that "everyone has the right to own property alone as well as in association with others" (Brownlie and Goodwin-Gill 2006, 26). Opposition by socialist states did not cause the exclusion of the right to own property from the later covenants, as might be assumed. Rather, discussion of private property during negotiation of the two covenants was bogged down in definitional questions. Additionally, those who advocated blanket protection of all private property could not come to an agreement with those who advocated protection of only enough personal property to ensure that citizens enjoyed a decent living (Schabas 1991).

Property-based market economies may be necessary both for economic growth and to permit individuals to exercise their own capabilities to support themselves, but they are not sufficient for economic human rights. Redistribution of wealth through taxes, income supplements, and welfare schemes is still necessary, even in the richest market economies. Redistribution should be an important aspect of government policy to ensure protection of the economic human rights of citizens who cannot fulfill their economic needs on their own and to ensure their possession of enough resources for a dignified life. Moreover, devoting public resources to the equitable and universal distribution of public goods such as education and health care in turn promotes economic growth as it creates a society with more productive citizens.

The emergence of a redistributive, welfare-oriented state depends on many political and social factors, including—most prominently—state guarantees of civil and political rights. The Bush administration agreed that these rights were necessary. "The key factor affecting whether or not nations develop is the extent to which they enjoy good governance which permits individuals to develop their talents and their intellects to the maximum extent, which allows them to speak and freely associate with one another, and which allows them to regularly choose their representatives in governments—in short, whether governments afford their people basic human rights" (Danies 2003). Civil and political rights increase the likelihood that governments will engage in accountable, transparent policymaking and devote resources to the economic human rights of their citizens.

The Bush administration did not advocate, however, that all human rights must be available to all sectors of society, so that they could protest against government policies and the very world market system that sometimes results in economic growth. Bush did not advocate rights for labor, nor did he advocate redistributive policies that would protect the poor. He disagreed explicitly with the principle of economic human rights, arguing that what the international regime called rights, such as the right to an adequate standard of living, were actually goals or aspirations, and that individuals should have the opportunities to achieve these goals via their own efforts (Weissbrodt 2006, 48). By contrast, I argue that states must pay attention to economic human rights at the same time as economies open up to the world market and at the same time as civil and political rights are entrenched. If globalization does result in better protection of human rights in the longer term, it will be as a result of very complex social and political processes, not as a result of simple and inevitable connections between the free market and human rights.

SIMPLE MODELS

Some commentators propose very simple relationships between globalization and human rights, implying that a positive relationship between the two is inevitable, as suggested by the following simple model:

$$\text{globalization} \rightarrow \text{human rights}$$

Much of the positive rhetoric surrounding globalization seems to refer to this relationship. Social actors do not have to do anything to promote human rights in societies experiencing globalization; human rights will "emerge," as it were, as societies globalize. Polanyi referred to a similar "utopian endeavor of economic liberalism to set up a self-regulating market system," in the belief that such a system would necessarily lead to liberal democracy and peace (1944, 29). This rhetoric assumes that simple economic interaction among societies will result in a merging of social and political values, without specifying what kind of contact among which social actors will result in positive, rights-inducing changes. There was and is, however, an underlying belief that wealthier societies are more likely to protect human rights than poorer societies, as illustrated by the simple model complicated:

$$\text{globalization} \rightarrow \text{wealth} \rightarrow \text{human rights}$$

Yet while wealthier societies do have more resources available to protect human rights, it is not necessarily the case that they will use their wealth for that purpose. Inequality and lack of redistributive measures may keep the poor poverty stricken or even render them worse off than before, especially if civil and political rights are also denied.

One version of the simple model complicated is the notion of "trickle-down" wealth creation, which became popular during the 1980s presidency of Ronald Reagan in the United States. According to this theory, whatever the short-term costs to the poor, in the longer term the wealth accrued by the rich will trickle down to them (Greiden 1981). During the first great transformation, however, wealth did not trickle down in a steady fashion to the poor. In response to impoverishment, the British government in the late eighteenth century introduced a set of regulations known as the Speenhamland Laws to provide for minimum subsistence for the poor. The introduction of these laws reflected the older social world of collective responsibility for all, although it was also a reaction against the dangers that large numbers of roving, impoverished people posed for an orderly society. In 1834 the government abolished the Speenhamland Laws, in part because employers believed that guaranteed provision of minimum subsistence deterred the poor from looking for work (Polanyi 1944, 101–2). This change in nineteenth-century British policy presaged debates in contemporary capitalist societies about what level of support should be given to the poor in order to provide them with minimum subsistence but not discourage them from finding work.

The new poor of the first great transformation did not overcome their miserable situation until they achieved universal male suffrage and the right to form trade unions. Despite these achievements, in Britain the period between 1834 and 1895 was one of horrific poverty in the midst of great wealth—the kind of poverty that preoccupied Karl Marx and Friedrich Engels and persuaded them of the need for working men's associations (trade unions), if not socialist revolution ([1888] 1967). Comprehensive minimum welfare provisions—what we now call economic rights—were not reintroduced in Britain until after World War II, following a strong victory by the Labor Party in the 1945 elections (Judt 2005, 74–75). The first great transformation thus suggests the need for a model of the relationship between globalization and human rights that takes political variables into account, hence the simple model further complicated:

globalization → markets → liberal economic order →
democracy → human rights

This yet more complicated version of the optimistic logic about the relationship between globalization and human rights specifies the factors that connect wealth to human rights. Globalization opens up markets; markets are the basis of the liberal economic order; the liberal economic order is the basis of democracy; democracy is the basis of human rights. Again, however, there is no necessary causation here; the relationships among these various factors are complex and nonlinear, circling back on one another and always running the risk of being blocked by negative economic changes or regressive social forces, as figure 4.1 shows.

A COMPLEX MODEL

Figure 4.1 is an ideal-type diagram of how globalization can sometimes promote human rights. It starts with one, and only one, change introduced into a country: namely, transnational investment. It assumes that the country is not democratic and does not respect human rights, but does permit DFI. Real-life examples are South Korea, Taiwan, and Singapore; these countries introduced capitalism and open, export-oriented economies in the mid-twentieth century but were still authoritarian and denied their citizens civil and political rights. Transnational investment in such countries, in this ideal-type model, produces some changes along the lines proposed by the engine of development school mentioned in chapter 1, which asserts that TNCs create jobs, provide employee benefits, and help create a middle class. The middle class, in its turn, becomes the political motor of democratization, demanding not only protection of its property rights but also those freedoms that allow it to prosper. Reverting to real-life examples, by the end of the twentieth century, South Korea and Taiwan had become democracies while Singapore remained autocratic.

The fact that some industrializing Asian states democratized in the late twentieth century and others did not suggests that the social and political

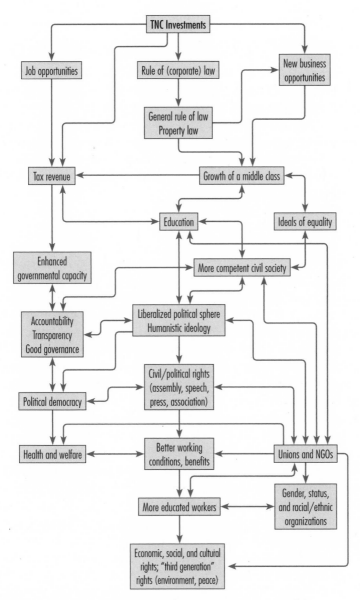

Figure 4.1   The Second Great Transformation: A Positive Model

changes that promote human rights, though encouraged by globalization, are not inevitable. All rights, especially economic rights, depend
upon social movements and political action. Whatever a theoretical model
might suggest about globalization's positive effects on economic rights,
only concrete social action will bring about these benefits. Nevertheless, it
is worth constructing a theoretical model of how this might occur.

On the economic front, the most obvious change in a society newly
encountering transnational investment is the creation of new employment and business opportunities. More people can make more money.
For example, many more women can enter paid employment; indeed,
"trade globalization has a generally positive influence on women's status"
(Richards and Gelleny 2007, 871). A small yet growing number of people
work in the modern, industrial sector. Some of these people pay taxes to
the government, as does the TNC itself unless it is allowed complete tax
exemption in perpetuity. Increased national revenue is associated with
improvement in human rights (Pritchard 1989). Higher national revenue improves governmental capacity: with more tax revenue, the government can pay its civil servants more regularly, giving them an incentive
to stay in their offices and abide by rules of fairness and impartiality,
rather than wander off to eke out a living in the informal sector or ask for
bribes every time a citizen makes a request.

New economic opportunities also lessen the likelihood that moves
toward political democracy will be resisted. Both political and bureaucratic officeholders will be less frightened by the possibility of losing
office if they can maintain their standard of living by moving to positions
in the private sector. This will reduce one of the chief causes of corruption among high-level officeholders: the fact that there are few economic
opportunities in the industrial, legal, and professional sectors to serve as
alternate sources of income if they lose office. Elites are also less likely to
resist democratization or foment coups d'état against existing democracies if the poorer sectors of the population earn more money. The more
prosperous the poor become by taking advantage of the new economic
opportunities offered by the globalized economy, the less likely they
will be to demand that the elites' property be redistributed via higher
taxes or outright confiscation. The larger the middle class created by

globalization, the more people will be willing to protect property rights and advocate lower taxes, thus reducing elites' interest in overthrowing democratic governments (Acemoglu and Robinson 2006, 321–48).

TNC investment also contributes to establishment of the rule of law. Investors want predictable laws and competent judicial systems to enforce their contracts and property rights. They do not want governments that renege on their contracts, as China was wont to do until very recently (Zhang 2008), or that are too weak or uninterested to enforce property laws, as in early postcommunist Russia (Miller and Tenev 2007; Polishchuk and Savvateev 2004). TNC investment results in more local business opportunities, either directly in relationship with the TNCs by supplying locally made inputs, for example, or indirectly by providing goods and services for workers who have established new communities in the regions of TNC investment. The new middle class that takes advantage of these opportunities desires protection and enforcement of its property and contracts.

Not only the rich but also the poor benefit when the law protects private property. One of the biggest stumbling blocks to development in Latin America, Asia, and Africa today is that the poor are frequently not legal owners of their houses, land, and mini-enterprises. Without legal title, they are at the mercy of corrupt bureaucrats who demand bribes, threatening to evict the poor from their homes and businesses if they do not pay. Furthermore, without evidence of legally enforced property rights, the poor have no collateral to offer banks for loans and often have to disperse their enterprises among many different locations to prevent seizure of their illegal assets (De Soto 2002). It is estimated that four billion people lack full legal identity, ranging from nonregistration at birth to lack of access to the courts, to lack of legal ownership of property. That "the vast majority of the world's people live outside the law . . . is a recipe for national and global stagnation" (Commission on Legal Empowerment of the Poor 2008, 10).

The new middle class also spurs demand for publicly provided social goods. While it may emerge from the ranks of those who are already educated, as did Chinese entrepreneurs from a socialist society that stressed education (Sen 1999, 42), this class will want even more opportunities for education so that its children can join their parents in business and later manage the property they inherit. The middle class may also desire a more educated general population so that businesses can employ individuals with the skills they need. TNCs may eventually join the demand for more education or provide their own educational systems if they discover that they need more literate and numerate workers.

As the new middle class becomes more aware of its own interests, it becomes less willing to live under the rule of traditional elders, intransigent bureaucracies, or autocratic dictators. It establishes the rudiments of a civil society, organizing to protect its own interests. This civil society in turn feeds back into the educational system, promulgating new ideas of the proper relationship between citizen and ruler. It promotes ideals of social equality to enhance its own chances of advancement regardless of the former or present social statuses of its members, and it enhances governmental capacity, demanding fairness and efficiency and displaying some willingness to pay taxes in order to obtain them. A more secure bureaucracy is more willing to listen and respond to citizens' concerns. As it does so, it learns that it is possible to make changes in policy, even to disburse more funds, without losing control of the state. Adhering to the principles of accountability and transparency—key aspects of good governance—is easier in state institutions that are properly funded and in which bureaucrats are well trained and adequately paid.

An emergent civil society also begins to demand a more liberalized political sphere in which citizens make their interests known and expect their government to take them into account. Citizens want the rule of law to extend beyond property and contract; they demand regularity, fairness, and predictability in other spheres of life. A government that is less reliant than it was previously on corruption and more accustomed to bureaucratic procedure is more willing to entertain the possibility of liberalizing—gradually granting freedoms of speech, press, and association that permit citizens to articulate their wishes.

A more humanistic ideology develops along with and as a partial cause of the more liberalized political sphere. As the market spreads and impersonal market relations become more common, commerce begins to take precedence over prejudice. Strangers become individuals with whom transactions are made, rather than bearers of unknown, often fear-inducing identities. A universal moral sense develops. Indeed, one might argue that the market breeds civility; all parties must communicate with one another in a tolerant fashion, and all must be willing to compromise if fair exchanges are to take place. The economic market affects the political market, as market trust helps to build the social trust necessary for a functioning democracy (Madison 1998, 152–57). Market relations and contract law impose a culture of promises, increasing the likelihood that individuals will honor their commitments to distant others (Haskell 1985, 551).

While the development of civil society and market trust makes it easier for the middle class to function in capitalist society, the entrenchment of economic rights for members of the working class requires a different and expanded set of social actors. Workers in the modern, industrialized sector try to organize independent trade unions that can act as their bargaining agents; to do so, they require the prior right of freedom of association. Attaining small, incremental improvements in working conditions emboldens them to ask for more rights. They also learn how to take part in large, bureaucratized organizations and how to lobby and bargain. They organize politically and demand that the state provide them with economic security in times of unemployment. In some countries, their demands become part of the platform of existing middle-class political parties; in other countries, workers organize their own new socialist or social democratic parties.

As workers become more educated and experienced, they enter other spheres of civil society, generalizing the idea that social benefits should be available to all citizens, whatever their status as entrepreneurs or workers; they particularly focus on education, health, and social welfare. Improvements in these spheres in turn spiral backward, affecting citizens' capacity to take part in political democracy. Both workers and members of the middle class, now living under the rudiments of the rule of law and political democracy, absorb the idea that with rights they are legally equal citizens of their country. This idea then spreads to other groups that have previously been excluded from the human rights discourse and treated as "natural" subordinates, such as women, persons occupying lower castes or statuses, or ethnic, religious, or racial minorities. These groups in turn form their own civic associations and learn the same lobbying and bargaining techniques as the middle and working classes.

The above is not so much a prediction as a rough description of what happened in western Europe and North America during and after the first great transformation, and in some Asian countries in the second half of the twentieth century. The introduction of capitalism resulted in the development of new social classes capable of pressuring governments to grant them civil and political rights. They then used their civil and political rights to demand economic rights. Following the example of the labor movement, civil rights and equality movements for other groups such as women, African Americans, and gays and lesbians also emerged. These groups in turn used their civil and political rights to demand enhanced access to jobs, property, equal opportunity, and economic rights.

None of the social changes just discussed were inevitable, however, nor did they occur in the West in a linear fashion. They spiraled back upon themselves again and again. Enhanced governmental capacity, for example, fed into education, which fed into employment, which fed into taxes, which fed back into enhanced governmental capacity. Moreover, there was downward as well as upward movement. Democratic Europe and North America fought a war against fascism in the 1940s; fascism was in part a reaction against the atomizing, competitive nature of the market economy, an attempt to reintroduce a circumscribed, racially or religiously based social world.

The social changes described in this chapter occurred during the first great transformation from agricultural to capitalist societies. This same transformation also characterizes much of the second great transformation (the exception is the move from socialist industrial societies to capitalist industrial societies in the former Soviet Union and Eastern Bloc). There is a strong connection between capitalism and democracy, but class action and organization are necessary for that connection to be established (Rueschemeyer, Stephens, and Stephens 1992). Members of previously downtrodden groups must mobilize and organize in order to force the rich and their representatives in government to grant rights to the poor. Studies of the relationship between economic development and human rights show that "economic development [usually capitalist] does not enhance directly political or civil rights," but that "social mobilization has a direct relationship with the expansion and contraction of political and civil rights" (Landman 2002, 920).

These connections confirm Sen's view that development depends on free human agency (1999, 4). Participatory freedoms are particularly important: "Political freedoms (in the form of free speech and elections) help to promote economic security. Social opportunities (in the form of education and health facilities) facilitate economic participation. Economic facilities (in the form of opportunities for participation in trade and production) can help to generate personal abundance as well as public resources for social facilities. Freedoms of different kinds can strengthen one another" (1999, 11).

Sen's account of the relationship among different kinds of freedoms supports Shue's theory of the relationship among different kinds of rights and the need for security (freedom of the person) to supplement subsistence (1980). Economic human rights cannot be guaranteed if citizens do not enjoy the right to make demands of the state or speak out against state policies that harm their material interests. Similarly, Fein concludes that "states that respect life integrity [rights such as protection against torture] enable their citizens to live longer and better than citizens of other states in the same region that are gross violators of human rights" (2007, 182). States that do not violate life integrity rights rely for support on political legitimacy rather than repressive coercion. They obtain legitimacy in part by investing in economic human rights, such as facilities for health, education, and sanitation, and allowing citizen participation. These, in turn, create more opportunities for civil society and social trust (Fein 2007, 190–91).

Democracy is "above all a matter of power"; subordinated classes must wrest democracy from the powerful (Rueschemeyer, Stephens, and Stephens 1992, 5). Class action in support of democracy and human rights does not occur in all societies, however. The actual historical experiences of various countries create the conditions that permit social movements to organize for democracy in some places but not others. Successful class action is facilitated especially by improvements in education and communication, as well as urbanization and the concentration of population. This results in the emergence of civil society as a counterweight to state power.

These social transformations are not inevitable. While "capitalist development is associated with democracy because it transforms the class structure" (Rueschemeyer, Stephens, and Stephens 1992, 7), as just described, there can certainly be capitalism without democracy. Alliances between old and new elite classes are possible, as between the old landlord class and the new business class in much of Latin America until the 1990s. That alliance permitted industrialization while blocking peasants and urban workers from deriving any benefits from the new system of wealth creation. Moreover, a governing elite can command resources such as decision-making power over investment and taxation, making it worthwhile for the international capitalist class to ally itself with that elite and blocking any changes that domestic lower classes might demand. Finally, the military can intervene in capitalist development, protecting both indigenous elites and foreign investors from internal worker or peasant unrest, as occurred when the military overthrew the socialist government of Chile on September 11, 1973.

Such blockage of the forces of democratization and human rights is just as much a prospect in the early twenty-first century as it was in the nineteenth and twentieth. The new global capitalism is not an exact replica of nineteenth-century Western capitalism. In Russia, for example, the rudimentary democracy installed just after the end of communism was transformed into an authoritarian system in which opposition political parties were administratively stymied in their attempts to capture public attention, and opponents of the incumbent regime who might have captured some public support were frequently imprisoned or murdered. Many Russian citizens preferred public order to the disrupted way of life they had endured during the transition to capitalism and looked back with longing to communism, which had supplied a modicum of economic security, at least to those who conformed to the Communist Party's political demands.

Thus, we cannot be sure that the happy model of the West's first great transformation will be an accurate representation of the second transformation—the spread of global capitalism into the farthest reaches of what were once isolated, and sometimes insulated, communist or peasant societies. We must also consider a negative ideal-type model of the present transformation.

5

NEGATIVE MODELS

Chapter 4 discussed the theoretical possibility that in the long term, globalization could improve human rights worldwide. This chapter presents the alternate theoretical view: namely, that globalization is more likely to adversely affect human rights in the long term. Following the organization of chapter 4, I discuss simple models of a possible negative connection between globalization and human rights, followed by a more complicated model. As in chapter 4, I present ideal types, so my negative models are not meant to represent any real cases. I began chapter 4 by discussing the case for a global market economy; I end chapter 5 by discussing the case against it, with reference especially to the 2008 world food crisis.

SIMPLE MODELS

Many critics think it obvious that globalization undermines human rights. Three successively more complicated models present the negative relationship between globalization and human rights, beginning with the following simple model:

globalization → rightlessness

The simple model assumes that globalization has only negative economic, social, and political effects. People are more likely to enjoy their human rights if they live in a locally, rather than globally, controlled environment. Globalization is "survival of the meanest" (Oloka-Onyango and Tamale 1995, 727), and the global economic regulatory system is "little more than a re-creation of the institutions of colonialism with a more friendly face" (Cavanagh and Mander 2004, 322). In this view, Western capitalists and political leaders use international organizations (IOs) such as the World Trade Organization (WTO) as agencies of "unofficial global government enforcing a corporate agenda" on states and citizens who cannot defend themselves against economic attack (Grierson, Lasn, and MacKinnon 1999–2000, 64).

Whereas supporters of globalization insert wealth as the intervening variable between globalization and human rights, its critics insert de-development, as illustrated by the simple model complicated:

$$\text{globalization} \rightarrow \text{de-development} \rightarrow \text{rightlessness}$$

These critics assume that by its very nature globalization will undermine development, not promote it. The ideal of development that they favor can be roughly described as including equitable distribution of wealth, ecologically sound investment (sustainable development), and nonexploitative social relationships, such as cooperative rather than profit-oriented production. Globalization's critics assume that without their opposition, the social changes and political processes induced by globalization will only further the interests of the already rich and powerful. Globalization, in their view, introduces a liberal economic order that creates a class society in which the gap between rich and poor is widened and, by virtue of their poverty, the poor suffer from rightlessness. This view is summarized in the simple model further complicated:

$$\text{globalization} \rightarrow \text{market economies} \rightarrow \text{liberal economic order} \rightarrow \text{class}$$
$$\text{society (rich vs. poor)} \rightarrow \text{rightlessness}$$

As discussed in chapter 4, capitalism does create societies divided among unequal social classes, and globalization is, above all, the worldwide spread of capitalism. Although the introduction of capitalism often results in a significant increase in national wealth, such an increase does not, in and of itself, imply more equitable distribution of resources, nor does it imply that social interaction will be nonexploitative. Usually, early capitalism implies the opposite. In many states that enter the global market economy, inequality does widen, sometimes severely, at least in the initial stages of growth. In the globalized world, the policies of transnational corporations (TNCs) often exacerbate the internal class divisions in societies that rely on the global marketplace. Thus, social class remains one of the most important determinants of full enjoyment of individual human rights in capitalist countries.

A COMPLEX MODEL

Critics argue that globalization forces the conditions of early western European capitalism onto an unwilling world, with states and TNCs colluding to deny rights to citizens and workers. TNCs, critics maintain, undercut local businesses when they invest in a country; underpay and mistreat workers; corrupt government officials; undermine the sustainability of the local communities where they operate; damage the environment; and prevent the organization of trade unions. They oppose social policies such as minimum wage laws, claiming that they constitute restrictions on free trade. In effect, critics argue, "corporate greed" (Arat 2006, 17) undermines national goals to protect and fulfill economic human rights. Many of these accusations are accurate, depending on the actual TNC, the circumstances under which it invests, and the attitudes of both the government where it is headquartered and the government that is host to its activities.

Globalization's critics often point out that some corporations' annual revenues are larger than the gross domestic products of many countries. Among such corporations, the top five in 2008 were Wal-Mart, Exxon Mobil, Royal Dutch Shell, BP (British Petroleum), and Toyota Motor, with revenues ranging respectively from $378.8 billion to $230.2 billion (Fortune Magazine 2008). In 2007 thirty-three countries had higher gross domestic products than Toyota Motor; these included fourteen non-Western countries, which in order of size were Japan, China, Brazil, the Russian Federation, India, the Republic of Korea, Mexico, Turkey, Indonesia, Saudi Arabia, South Africa, Iran, Argentina, and Thailand, with gross domestic products ranging respectively from $4.376 trillion to $245.8 billion (World Bank 2008b). Thus, it is not entirely true that TNCs dominate the world economy at the expense of non-Western or developing states.

While oil contributed to the wealth of some of these non-Western countries, including the Russian Federation, Indonesia, Saudi Arabia, and Iran, much of their wealth was due to their participation in the global economy. Moreover, while most large TNCs were based in Western countries or Japan, some were emerging in the early twenty-first century in formerly underdeveloped parts of the world, especially China and India (*Economist* 2007b, 78). These facts illustrate the significant restructuring of the world economy that took place in the 1990s and early twenty-first century. This restructuring, however, does not necessarily mean that in the long run the world's poor will benefit from globalization.

The positive model of the connections between TNC investment and human rights presented in chapter 4 was based largely on the historical model of capitalist development in western Europe and North America. Yet the globalization of capitalism in the twenty-first century may not result in the spread of democracy and civil and political rights, much less the spread of economic human rights. In this section, I reverse the positive model of the possible connection between human rights and globalization, this time starting with hot money investment as opposed to the productive investment at the core of the positive model.

A key difference between the earlier evolution in western Europe of capitalist, democratic, and eventually rights-protective societies and the economic changes occurring in the twenty-first century is the role of international financial institutions (IFIs). IFI decisions that restrict the space for sovereign policymaking and for political negotiation between a state's government and its citizens can reduce the likelihood that human rights will be attained. Thus, I have added decisions by IFIs, a factor excluded from figure 4.1 (the positive model), to figure 5.1. This pessimistic model is extrapolated in part from Stiglitz's description of the

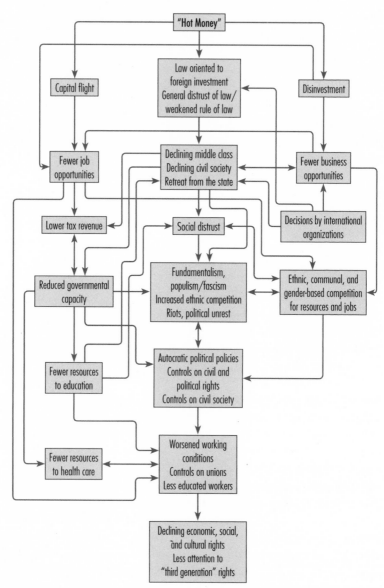

Figure 5.1 The Second Great Transformation: A Pessimistic Model

Asian economic meltdown of 1997 (2002, 89–132). I enlarge Stiglitz's analysis to a more general model of how a society that is both growing economically and becoming more politically open can regress. This is a short-term picture, not a long-term prognosis; indeed, by 2002 the Asian economic crisis was "receding into the past" (Friedman 2002, 52). Nevertheless, it serves to show that the optimistic picture of globalization, based upon a retrospective reading of how western Europe and North America developed, is not necessarily the only model of economic, social, and political evolution for the twenty-first century.

In the pessimistic model of the second great transformation, TNCs are once again the principal agents of change, but in this case they are not long-term investors; rather, they are hot money short-term investors. When an economic crisis occurs in a country, hot money investors withdraw their assets as quickly as possible. Without capital, local businesses cannot pay their debts and many fail. There are fewer jobs, both within the foreign investment sector and the local sector of businesses and professions geared to servicing foreign-owned businesses and the foreigners themselves. Additionally, the middle class's savings are reduced as foreign disinvestment results in lower valuations on locally owned investments.

With increased local indebtedness, fewer local jobs, and lower personal savings, the government's tax revenue declines and, consequently, so does overall government capacity. The government cuts the number of civil servants and reduces funds to health and education. As local workers become less healthy and less educated, the country becomes less attractive to future investors. Whatever democratization and development of civil society might have previously occurred is now subject to threat. Society begins to distrust the rule of law as it becomes obvious that it has been used to protect the interests of hot money investors. Distrust in the rule of law generates distrust in government as an institution capable of reforming a disintegrating economy. With declining or no faith in government, communities and individuals retreat from the state, seeking ways to support themselves without reliance on public officials.

Distrust in law and government expands into generalized social distrust; far from civilizing social relations, the unregulated, every-man-for-himself market separates individuals from one another and society.

Ethnic and communal groups start to compete for jobs, business opportunities, and government benefits. Men try to force women back into
the home, away from the economic opportunities that helped women
emancipate themselves from men's control. Food riots and other political demonstrations manifest extreme social unrest. Political parties based
upon conservative interpretations of how society should be organized, or
parties advocating militant and sometimes violent solutions to political
crisis, quickly arise, recruiting especially among unemployed young men.
Political and religious leaders exploit the crisis, sometimes introducing a
politics of resentment against the West, which is attractive to those who
believe that some of their problems result from policies imposed on their
governments by Western-dominated IFIs. Minority ethnic groups with
strong ties to the international capitalist system are particularly at risk.

Such economic and social crises often cause a reversion from democracy to autocracy. As they attempt to meet outside economic demands to
pay their debts and simultaneously restore internal civic order, governments impose controls on civil and political rights and civil society. In an
effort to draw international hot money and capital back into the country,
they offer a weakened labor force, imposing stricter controls on trade
unions. Less educated than before and less able to exercise their basic
civil and political rights, workers have less leverage in pressuring governments and employers for their economic rights, which consequently
decline. Third generation rights, such as the right to a clean environment, also suffer without civil society organization to promote them.

Thus, hot money capital flight unleashes a long chain of detrimental
consequences for countries entering the global capitalist economy. Capital flight, however, is not the only way in which globalization can cause
economic decline and political degeneration. General market relations
can have the same effect.

SOVEREIGNTY, SOCIALITY, AND SUBSISTENCE

The global market can have many positive effects. In chapter 2, I presented evidence that the rate of world poverty has been declining, in

large part because China and India have entered the global marketplace; by contrast, poverty is worst in those countries least able to enter. Nevertheless, as critics of globalization argue, entry into the world market can entail substantial costs, which may be summarized theoretically as loss of national sovereignty, loss of communal sociality, and loss of individual and collective subsistence.

In the late twentieth century, governments that accepted IFI advice to enter the world market on the "free" competitive terms discussed in chapter 3 sacrificed part of their sovereignty. While all states are legally sovereign and therefore technically entered into relationships with IFIs of their own accord, many governments' choices were highly constrained. Financial assistance or debt relief was usually conditioned on structural adjustment policies (SAPs). States that adopted SAPs did sacrifice some of their sovereignty in practice, if not in principle, as IOs over which they often had little influence made key decisions that affected them (McGrew 1998). States became accountable to suprastate bodies in ways that had not existed in the past (Freeman 2002, 155).

When such states entered into agreements in the World Trade Organization (WTO), for example, they often did so with weak bargaining power and a lack of the technical and legal resources they needed for disputes with more powerful states (Ostry 2009). Many smaller countries had no permanent representatives at the WTO, while the United States had hundreds of negotiators (Evans 2001, 98–99). In any case, "enforcement [of WTO rules] is asymmetric—a threat of trade restriction by the United States against a small country like Antigua will elicit a response, but the United States does not pay much attention if Antigua threatens a trade restriction" (Stiglitz 2006, 76). Thus, the United States could punish a small country that violated WTO rules by restricting its trade with that country, but a small country could not punish the United States in the same way.

This sacrifice of state sovereignty also frequently undermined the democracy that IFIs and Western states claimed to be advocating for previously undemocratic developing countries. SAP conditionality required governments to make decisions that their citizenry often opposed, causing a democratic deficit (Sandbrook 2000, 1077). In the early period of

SAPs, governments were advised not to offer universal free primary education or health care, as these drained national budgets, yet education and health care were two of the most important goods that governments could deliver to their citizens. These policies weakened the sovereign right of governments to decide how best to serve their citizens. Thus, the wave of democratization of the 1990s sometimes occurred in a substantive vacuum; citizens could choose their leaders, but they could not choose the policies they wanted their leaders to implement. In effect, sovereignty was no longer tied to territory; it was now tied to function (Goodhart 2005, 29–47). Undemocratic, nonaccountable IFIs had taken over one of the most important functions of the modern state: overseeing economic policy.

The second sacrifice, the loss of sociality, was one of the key aspects of the first great transformation on which Polanyi remarked (1944). In kin- and village-based societies, individuals rarely suffered anomie, a sense of disconnection from the wider society (Durkheim 1951, 241–76). Their lives were always enmeshed—for better or worse—in complex social relations. Individuals had a sense of belonging to the group, even when their social roles, such as young man, woman, or child, subordinated them to male heads of households or local authorities. They had a clear sense of who they were and what was expected of them; social norms were commonly known, and communal rituals and festivals reinforced the sense of belonging.

This sense of belonging, however, should not be romanticized. Those with higher status and authority often discriminated against outsiders, persons of lower castes, slaves, and others. For example, in many societies women who lived without the "protection" of a man were—and still are—vulnerable to the charge of being witches. Those men who controlled more land or other forms of wealth than others, or who had more wives and children, frequently engaged in severe economic exploitation of their subordinates; these local authorities also manipulated religious or mystical roles and knowledge in their own interests. Many people therefore fled the preindustrial social world when they had the chance, in order to escape from the dark underside of status-bound and rule-bound sociality.

Much of the loss of sociality in the contemporary world is a consequence not of late twentieth-century globalization but of the earlier change from rural, agricultural society to urbanized, industrial society that has occurred in most of the former global south since at least 1950. It also resulted from autonomous decisions made by national governments pursuing modernization policies. Individuals pursuing perceived improvements in their life chances likewise made autonomous decisions to withdraw from the sociality of rural life. Some preferred the privacy of urban life, where they could pursue their own life choices without interference from family or neighbors. Others escaped their demeaned village status by moving to urban areas where it was not known that they were originally from lower castes or were of slave ancestry. Nevertheless, the "great disruption" (Fukuyama 1999)—the shift from social embeddedness to social choice—often caused psychological hardship in the global south, as it did earlier in the Western world. This hardship was intensified by the end of assured minimum subsistence, the third sacrifice made by some states, communities, and individuals entering the global economy.

In some precapitalist societies, authorities took minimal responsibility for the people's welfare, or as much as they could in situations of permanent scarcity. In parts of Africa, for example, chiefs were expected to ensure that everyone in the village had enough land to cultivate food for his or her family. In the more egalitarian and collectively responsible of such societies, scarcity was shared, as was abundance; reciprocity and redistribution took precedence over market profitability (Sandbrook 2000, 1075). Markets, if they existed, were local and small scale, limited to exchanges of goods in which villages specialized.

Again, however, precapitalist and noncapitalist rural societies should not be romanticized. In many, men and boys had a greater chance of guaranteed subsistence than women and girls, who commonly ate last and worst (Sen 1990). Those who occupied low social status, such as slaves or members of lower castes, were also less likely to have access to food than those of high social status. In Mauritania, freed slaves in the late twentieth century frequently found that "freedom means starvation," while those who remained slaves depended on their masters' often capricious kindness for food (Bales 1999, 87).

Peasant agriculture is often less productive than large-scale farming (Lewis 2008, 31). Nevertheless, converting all food supplies into marketable commodities can put intolerable strain on individuals who previously relied on local redistributive or protective measures to ensure at least a modicum of food in times of scarcity. "Free choice in the market is a sad joke for people so poor that they have nothing left to sell but their labour, their last plot of land, or their daughter" (Sandbrook 2000, 1076). In his early work on famines, Sen blamed much food scarcity on imperfect markets. Noting that famines often occur when there is only a small reduction in the food supply, he argued that scarcity could be alleviated by the free movement of food from surplus to scarce areas (1999, 160–88). Sen's work suggests that a market economy helps to avert famine. In the global economy, however, the market for food is international and those in need of food are often not in a position to buy it. Moreover, if the global market is distorted, food may not reach willing buyers. This is one aspect of what seems to have happened to the global food market in 2008.

THE 2008 WORLD FOOD CRISIS

In the first four months of 2008, the world experienced a food crisis during which the prices of basic staples rose drastically. Between March 2007 and March 2008, the price of rice rose by nearly 90 percent, wheat by 130 percent, maize (corn) by nearly a third, vegetable oil by 97 percent, and dairy products by 58 percent (Fleshman 2008, 12). In El Salvador— only one example of many countries hard hit by price increases—the poor were eating only half as much food in April 2008 as they had been a year earlier (*Economist* 2008c, 33). Food riots occurred in several countries, among them Egypt, Haiti, Cameroon, and Somalia (*Economist* 2008c, 31; Associated Press 2008). It was feared that this food price inflation, which might push one hundred million more people into poverty in 2008 (*Economist* 2008c, 33), would undermine much of the progress made in the late twentieth century in reducing child malnutrition. While 47.1 percent of children under five in developing countries were malnourished to the point of stunting (manifesting low height for their age group) in 1980, by 1990 that figure had declined to 39.8 percent and by 2005 to 29 percent (de Onis, Frongillo, and Blossner 2000, 1226).

The causes of these extraordinary increases in the price of food were very complex and included temporary environmental events such as severe drought in Australia and the unprecedented high price of oil in the first four months of 2008 (Ban 2008). The price of diesel fuel, used to transport food, also increased (Surk 2008). The price of fertilizers rose dramatically. Increased wealth in countries like China was another cause: as Chinese citizens became wealthier, they ate more meat, especially pork. As more grain goes to feeding animals, less grain and land are available to feed humans (*Economist* 2007a, 81). Finally, much land previously used for food crops was converted to production of biofuels in response to the rising price of oil (Organisation for Economic Co-operation and Development 2007, 3).

Distortions in national and international food markets also contributed to the food crisis. One such distortion was rich-country subsidies of biofuel production, which depleted the amount of land devoted to food crops (*Economist* 2008e, 13). Another was the subsidies paid each year to European farmers, amounting to 55 billion euros in 2007 (*Economist* 2008d, 15), as well as those paid to American farmers. Ironically, in the 1950s these subsidies enabled American farmers to produce food that their government then exported to help feed the world's poor (Lewis 2008, 33), but by the twenty-first century the subsidies made the price of American foodstuffs so cheap that farmers in poorer countries could not compete and gave up producing food. Mexican corn producers, for example, could not compete with the highly subsidized American corn that flooded Mexican markets after the North American Free Trade Agreement came into effect in the 1990s (Bello 2008, 16). American food aid also undermined farmers in poor countries, who could not compete with the "free" food from the United States (*New York Times* 2008).

Because food had become so cheap in the late twentieth century, the world's richer countries and the IFIs had reduced investment in food research institutes. The result, especially for rice, was that new strains resistant to insects were no longer being developed or, if developed, were no longer stored (Bradsher and Martin 2008). Thus, farmers had fewer available resources to help them switch crops if one crop failed. All of these factors, combined with short-term environmental effects that, because of global climate change, might actually presage much longer-term effects, came to a head in early 2008.

Reactions to the food crisis exacerbated it. In March 2008 several countries, including Cambodia, Indonesia, and Argentina, restricted food exports, causing prices to rise further as the quantity of food available on the international market declined (*Economist* 2008a, 98). Simultaneously, investors began to speculate in food commodities, also driving up prices (Stiglitz 2008, A17). While no controls were imposed on financial speculation in food, the IFIs urged individual countries not to impose protectionist measures. One American official estimated that by March 2008, restrictions on wheat exports might have increased its wholesale price by 20 percent, while restrictions on rice exports from Asia helped raise its world price by 75 percent (*Economist* 2008a, 98). Nevertheless, there was no unanimity on the need to free exports or reduce subsidies; as late as May 2008, the French government argued in the EU that rising food prices meant governments should continue subsidizing European farmers to produce food staples (Kanter and Castle 2008).

The effects of the world food crisis were further aggravated by earlier transformation of formerly protected peasant economies into free market economies that relied principally on their comparative advantage in the international market to support themselves, in accordance with the advice of the International Monetary Fund (IMF). Once again using the methodology of ideal types, I propose a hypothetical situation in figure 5.2 to show how loss of sovereignty, sociality, and subsistence-based economies might have exacerbated the food crisis in some countries. I have named the hypothetical state in this illustration Coffeestan. Coffee is a common export crop; "stan" suggests the subordinate nature of most coffee-exporting countries in the world economy. I assume that Coffeestan's government is not dictatorial or autocratic; rather, it is a democracy trying to do the best it can for its citizens.

In Coffeestan, peasants used to produce food crops for their own subsistence and for the domestic market, but IFIs encouraged the state to

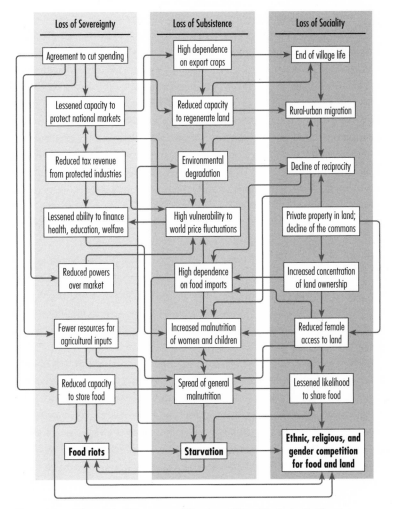

Loss of Sovereignty

Agreement to cut spending

Lessened capacity to protect national markets

Reduced tax revenue from protected industries

Lessened ability to finance health, education, welfare

Reduced powers over market

Fewer resources for agricultural inputs

Reduced capacity to store food

Food riots

Loss of Subsistence

High dependence on export crops

Reduced capacity to regenerate land

Environmental degradation

High vulnerability to world price fluctuations

High dependence on food imports

Increased malnutrition of women and children

Spread of general malnutrition

Starvation

Loss of Sociality

End of village life

Rural-urban migration

Decline of reciprocity

Private property in land; decline of the commons

Increased concentration of land ownership

Reduced female access to land

Lessened likelihood to share food

Ethnic, religious, and gender competition for food and land

Figure 5.2   Schematic Summary of Food and Free Trade in Coffeestan

instead produce coffee for the international market. Coffeestan enjoyed an international comparative advantage in coffee, and the IFIs assumed that by pursuing this comparative advantage it would earn enough foreign exchange to import the subsistence foods its citizens needed but no longer produced. Persuaded by IFI advice to integrate into the global market, Coffeestan abandoned protectionist measures on food production and distribution and encouraged its citizens to produce cash crops for the international market, rather than food crops for the local market.

Coffeestan relinquished part of its economic sovereignty in order to qualify for loans and grants from IFIs. It agreed to cut government spending, including spending on agricultural inputs it hitherto had provided to its farmers at subsidized prices; thus, its farmers were forced into the world market to obtain fertilizers. Coffeestan also agreed to stop protecting its infant industries, which had been a source of tax revenue (Stiglitz 2006, 72). Reduced tax revenue combined with IFI pressures to cut spending meant that Coffeestan reduced expenditures on health and education. Coffeestan's less educated and unhealthier population became less able to adjust to market changes, less able to take advantage of nonagricultural economic opportunities, and less able to innovate in order to compete with other coffee producers.

Coffestan had relinquished some of its powers to regulate its internal market so as to conform to the IFIs' notions of a perfect international free market in which, theoretically, it would be able to buy food at the market-induced lowest price. In so doing it became less able to purchase food to store to avert famine, and less able to provide basic welfare support for those who could not buy their own food. Thus, the government sacrificed its redistributive role as the last-resort source of food for its citizens to a market ideology that claimed, erroneously, that its citizens would always be able to purchase the food they needed as long as borders were open to trade.

The loss of sociality in Coffeestan exacerbated the food crisis. Prior to the state's adoption of an SAP, several decades of social change had already weakened social norms of redistribution and reciprocity. Village life was disrupted as many people, especially young men, migrated to urban areas. In the 1990s IFIs encouraged privatization of land so that ownership rights would be clear; they argued that owners, knowing that their private property was protected, would be more likely to invest in production for the international market. The new policy, however, meant that land increasingly passed into the hands of national and local elites, such as former military rulers and local headmen who usurped property from the less powerful. The notion of land as common property to be redistributed by local authorities as need dictated fell out of favor. Women lost their rights to use land to cultivate food crops for themselves and their children; sometimes their husbands sold the land to outside entrepreneurs, leaving the women and children without food. Land was no longer left fallow to regenerate; rather, it was increasingly overused to produce coffee.

In general, then, Coffeestan's new policy of producing cash crops for the world market undermined local subsistence. Coffeestan was extremely vulnerable to fluctuations in the price of the coffee it exported and the price of the foods it now imported. The production of coffee resulted in environmental degradation, so that it was difficult for Coffeestan's peasant cultivators to revert to food crop production when they could no longer buy imported foods. Without access to land of their own and without the capacity to purchase food on the international market, women and children were the first to feel the effects of reduced food supply, but they were not the only ones. When men also began experiencing food shortages, riots broke out. The government's incapacity to provide food weakened its democratic legitimacy. As access to food declined, gender-based, religious, and ethnic competition for food intensified. All of this was seriously aggravated by the earlier effects of desertification and loss of forested areas, as well as more recent global climate change that reduced the supply of fresh water and cultivable land.

The hypothetical story of Coffeestan is meant to show how some policies encouraged by IFIs and policies generally characteristic of market economies may have contributed to the 2008 world food crisis. Citizens of rich states might have experienced food price increases as annoying, but temporary, upward blips in what they paid at the grocery store, but citizens of poverty-stricken states starved. In April 2008 the *Economist* reported that "the middling poor, those on $2 a day, are pulling children from school and cutting back on vegetables so they can still afford rice. Those on $1 a day are cutting back on meat, vegetables and one or two meals, so they can afford one bowl. The desperate—those on 50 cents a day—face disaster" (2008e, 13).

By late 2008, the world food crisis was somewhat ameliorated; food prices fell again, partly due to the simultaneous fall in the price of oil. Nevertheless, food producers in poorer countries were still at the mercy of an unpredictable and fluctuating world market that affected both what they could sell and what they could buy. Furthermore, additional economic disasters occurred in 2008. In September the world capitalist economy suddenly entered a tailspin, caused in large part by the unregulated nature of financial products, as discussed in chapter 3. This crisis had immediate and perhaps long-term detrimental effects on the entire global economy, exacerbating the earlier effects of the food and oil price hikes.

In such a situation, retreat from the world capitalist market might seem a sensible strategy for sovereign states to adopt, given that for some countries the results of several decades of integration into that market seemed to have been nothing but impoverishment. The policy of Soviet-style socialism, although discredited, might become an attractive alternative to voters in new democracies; so also might populist measures meant to protect the citizenry against any incursion by the West or any attempt at modernization. In chapters 8 and 9, I discuss these possible political reactions to globalization. Before doing so, however, I discuss in chapters 6 and 7 some countervailing tendencies within globalization that may help alleviate some of its negative effects.

6

GLOBAL HUMAN RIGHTS GOVERNANCE

Human rights are frequently regarded only as dependent consequences of globalization: globalization affects human rights, but human rights do not affect globalization. Yet the principles, laws, and practices of global human rights governance independently affect both elite implementation of globalization and social action in favor of or against it. A major difference between the first and second great transformations is the existence the second time around of the international human rights regime and the international human rights social movement.

The concept of human rights has leapfrogged across time and space. While the ideals and laws of universal, individual human rights were introduced late in the evolution of Western capitalism, they were already part of the international scene before many of the world's poorer countries started to develop; thus, they leaped chronologically from early to late capitalism. Moreover, although the principle of human rights was first formally articulated in the Western world, it is now relevant everywhere; in that sense, it has leaped geographically over oceans and seas to affect domestic policy in nearly every country. From almost universal human rights lawlessness, global governance has evolved to universal human rights law. The principles supported by human rights laws have strong normative value, even when states attempt to sidestep them or ignore the very human rights treaties they sign. Human rights obligations are increasingly imposed on international organizations (IOs) and private corporate actors as well as states, although they are not yet strong enough to seriously constrain their behavior.

WESTERN DEVELOPMENT AND HUMAN RIGHTS LAWLESSNESS

The happy predictions made in figure 4.1, the optimistic ideal-type model of the second great transformation, rely on similarities to the social evolution of western Europe, North America, and parts of East Asia. Such similarities do not necessarily suggest an easy or inevitable transition of the rest of the world to wealthy, democratic, and rights-respecting societies, however. Formerly colonized countries do not have access to one of the most important economic advantages the West had during its own period of capitalist growth: namely, human rights lawlessness. Governments and employers were, by and large, not concerned about the rights of citizens and workers, nor were they concerned about the rights of those inhabiting the worlds they conquered. Uninhibited by human rights considerations, they could act entirely for their own economic benefit.

During the West's period of growth, no international law prevented the purchase or theft of people. Enslavement was a normal activity of the precapitalist and early capitalist periods; indeed, international law did not officially abolish slavery until 1926 (League of Nations 1926). Furthermore, no international law prohibited colonialism until 1960 (Du Plessis 2003, 657; Brownlie and Goodwin-Gill 2006, 45–47). Colonial conquest was a common practice inherited from the ancient world; it permitted Europeans to take over territories previously not part of the world economy and curtail or distort their economies as they saw fit.

During the period of Western expansion, moreover, there were no laws against massive population transfers. The ordinary inhabitants of Europe had few rights. Their governments could deport them to the colonies if they disobeyed the myriad laws that regulated their behavior, or deprive them of the lands they traditionally owned, as in the enclosure movement. Similarly, no international law prohibited ethnic cleansing or—until 1948—genocide (United Nations General Assembly [1948] 2006). Although some Catholic missionaries protested the maltreatment of aboriginal populations in the Americas, by and large colonists could do as they pleased to wipe out the "primitive" populations occupying territories they sought (Jones 2006, 70–76).

None of these economic advantages of human rights lawlessness, however, assured the prosperity of the Western world. Not all slave-trading states become equally wealthy, as Portugal demonstrates: an early slave-trading power, it fell behind other European states in the competition for economic growth. Nor did all colonial powers prosper equally; despite Spain's early colonization of the Americas, in economic growth it lagged far behind Britain, France, and several other countries that did not possess colonies (Wallerstein 1980, 179–85). The sorts of social changes diagramed in figure 4.1 were far more important to Western capitalist development than the slave trade or colonialism. Internal changes in habits, laws, entrepreneurial activities, and relations among social groups were necessary determinants of capitalist growth. Moreover, while many states, capitalists, and ruling classes prospered under conditions of human rights lawlessness, ordinary people in the exploiting states often did not. They had to engage in a protracted struggle for their human rights, just as citizens of newly industrializing countries do today.

In the globalized world now constrained by international human rights law, less developed countries adopting capitalism will be at some disadvantage in the search for economic growth compared to their Western predecessors. In particular, developing countries do not have the option of expelling "surplus" populations of unemployable young men or encouraging them to move to colonies, as did the Western powers. On the other hand, ordinary citizens of these less developed countries have an advantage, at least in legal terms, that citizens of the West did not enjoy well into the twentieth century. Both international law and many national constitutions stipulate that they cannot be expected to wait for their rights until their countries develop.

THE INTERNATIONAL HUMAN RIGHTS REGIME

Globalization refers not only to economic changes but also to political, governance, and legal changes; the international human rights regime is one of globalization's legal aspects. A regime is a system of "norms and decision-making procedures accepted by states as binding in a particular issue area" (Donnelly 2003, 127). The human rights regime is supraterritorial (Scholte 2002, 44): the rules exist above the level of the state, so long as each state agrees to them. States voluntarily dilute their sovereignty in favor of international treaties and regulations.

Both the reach and depth of international human rights law have grown significantly in the post–World War II period, especially since the 1970s. The international human rights regime now constrains the entire world, and most countries formally claim to respect its norms and laws. In principle, the regime means that neither rich nor poor countries may ignore their citizens' economic human rights. The argument that economic growth requires a free hand for governments and private entrepreneurs without regard to the well-being of citizens or those affected by corporate activities has little purchase in the early twenty-first century.

In the early decades after the UN proclaimed the 1948 Universal Declaration of Human Rights (UDHR), there were debates about the appropriateness of both the chronological and geographical leapfrogging of human rights. One debate concerned whether citizens should forego civil and political rights until after economic development had occurred. By the mid-1990s, this chronological debate had ended; except for a few holdouts, most governments acknowledged in principle that without civil and political rights, development might not occur, could be undermined, or could be skewed toward some sectors of the population and against others. Thus, governments accepted civil and political rights as necessary, regardless of a country's stage of development.

The debate about human rights leapfrogging geographically had also abated by the 1990s. Prior to that decade, scholars and politicians claiming to be spokespersons of various parts of the underdeveloped world commonly argued that human rights were a culturally relative concept. According to these commentators, human rights originated in the West and reflected its culture, especially its tendency to encourage individualism over collectivism and to prioritize human rights over social duties. Critics from Africa, Asia, the Islamic world, and indigenous communities variously argued that their more communitarian, duty-oriented perspectives were uniquely African, Asian, Islamic, or indigenous. The similarities of these regional arguments were rooted in nostalgia for their preindustrial, still heavily rural societies (Howard 1995, 79–108). As they entered the industrial world, even before the changes induced by globalization, sustaining these preindustrial societies became ever more difficult.

Even if the concept of human rights had originally been rooted in the philosophical speculations of eighteenth- and nineteenth-century Europe, the changes that accompanied globalization now meant that it applied to the entire world. Just as eighteenth- and nineteenth-century Europeans needed philosophical and legal defenses against the increasing powers of the state and the market, in the twentieth and twenty-first centuries individuals all over the world needed philosophical and legal defenses against both their own states and the local and international market economy. Thus, human rights leapfrogged over space as well as time.

By 2008 most countries had ratified the two major UN human rights covenants. Any state can sign a UN document, but ratification means that its provisions become part of the state's domestic law. One hundred and sixty-two countries ratified the International Covenant on Civil and Political Rights (ICCPR), and 159 ratified the International Covenant on Economic, Social, and Cultural Rights (ICESCR). The United States and China, however, were significant exceptions to the trend. The United States ratified the ICCPR in 1992, but as of 2008 had not ratified the ICESCR, although it signed it in 1977. China ratified the ICESCR in 2001, but by 2008 had not ratified the ICCPR, although it signed it in 1998. Moreover, China put a reservation on article 8 of the ICESCR, the article that protects trade union rights, stating that it had to be consistent with the Chinese Constitution: Chinese law does not permit trade unions independent of state control (Human Rights Watch 2008, 3).

The United States and China were extreme cases. In many other states, the interconnectedness of all types of human rights was no longer a matter of debate. By the late twentieth century, many, if not most, countries also included some statements about human rights in their national constitutions, indicating their acceptance of human rights, at least in principle. In that sense, human rights leapfrogging had been successful. States that incorporated human rights into their constitutions could no longer argue that for chronological reasons (their stage of development) or geographical reasons (their unique culture) their citizens did not need human rights. The global ideal of human rights was almost fully global in law. The incorporation of human rights law into domestic jurisdictions also meant that those states that had ratified the relevant covenants were obliged to report their progress on civil and political rights and economic, social, and cultural rights to the relevant UN monitoring bodies (Mertus 2005, 82). While these UN bodies had no power to force states to change their practices, they could use their influence through public criticism to embarrass or shame states into improving their records.

Thus, by the early twenty-first century, the ideals and law of human rights had become one aspect of global governance. States that ratified human rights documents ceded part of their sovereignty to the new global regime. While enforcement of human rights laws was weak, moral suasion did have an effect on some states and was often used to counter the detrimental effects of economic globalization. In addition, the first decade of the twenty-first century witnessed several serious efforts to codify human rights obligations of transnational corporations (TNCs) and international financial institutions (IFIs).

HUMAN RIGHTS OBLIGATIONS OF TRANSNATIONAL CORPORATIONS

Critics of globalization often claim that the international human rights regime controls states, yet the most influential global actors are uncontrolled TNCs. However, TNCs are not the only types of enterprise that can violate human rights; domestically owned private businesses and state-owned enterprises (SOEs) are also frequent violators. Nevertheless, public protest and human rights advocacy tend to target Western-owned TNCs rather than TNCs not based in the West, SOEs, or domestic businesses.

Critics focus especially on U.S.-based TNCs, which seem to violate human rights with impunity. American courts are quite conservative about imposing human rights obligations on TNCs, generally ruling that American corporations are not obliged to provide the same level of care in foreign countries as at home. For example, the pesticide DBCP causes sterility in men; its use was outlawed within the United States in 1977, but as of 2005 several American corporations, among them Dow Chemical and Del Monte Foods, still used it in their foreign operations without penalty by U.S. courts (Gibney 2005, 19–28). That the world's largest economic actor so disregards the human rights of those who are not its own citizens bodes ill for imposition of human rights obligations on TNCs. Nevertheless, the United States does allow foreigners who consider themselves victims of human rights violations to sue American corporations in American jurisdictions under its Alien Tort Claims Act; more than forty such cases had been brought to court by 2007 (Ruggie 2007, par. 30). Fewer legal protections exist for victims of human rights violations by TNCs based in some other countries, especially newly industrializing countries, than for victims of TNCs based in the United States.

No binding international law stipulates a code of human rights conduct for TNCs (Forsythe 2006, 232), although many soft-law regulatory norms had evolved by the early 2000s (Ruggie 2007, pars. 45–62). The UN and its affiliated agencies have been involved for some time in a campaign to persuade TNCs to adopt human rights obligations. In 1988 the International Labor Organization (ILO) issued a modest Declaration of Fundamental Principles and Rights at Work: these rights include freedom of association, the effective recognition of the right to collective bargaining, the elimination of all forms of forced or compulsory labor, the effective abolition of child labor, and the elimination of discrimination in employment (Brownlie and Goodwin-Gill 2006, 571). Yet in actual practice, corporations continue to stymie trade unions' freedom of association, and unions are often banned in developing countries' export processing zones (EPZs), special zones dedicated to production of exports for the international market (Gibb 2003, 61). Nor do voluntary codes or ILO documents generally protect the right to strike as opposed to the right to collective bargaining, yet the strike is workers' key weapon and the threat of strike one of the strongest bargaining tools they possess.

In 1999 the UN formulated a Global Compact to which corporations could voluntarily adhere. Businesses were asked to agree that they would respect international human rights, especially the ILO's fundamental principles, and "make sure that they are not complicit in human rights abuses." The Compact also asked them to adhere to several principles meant to protect the environment, and to take initiatives that would prevent corruption (United Nations 2007). By 2007, 3,800 businesses were members of the Global Compact (Wells 2008, 16), including 108 companies on the Financial Times Global 500 list (UN Global Compact Office 2007). However, this was a small percentage of the roughly 77,000 TNCs worldwide (Ruggie 2007, par. 64). Furthermore, some critics argued, the Global Compact was merely a public relations exercise, allowing corporations to forestall formulation of legally binding codes of conduct (Cavanaugh and Mander 2004, 282). The Global Compact provided a form of "blue-washing," associating corporations with the UN while shielding them from attention to their violations of human rights. Meanwhile, many were derelict even in their minimal obligations to periodically report their conduct to the Global Compact Office, and even those that clearly did not adhere to the Compact's standards were rarely sanctioned (Wells 2008).

In 2003 the UN Sub-Commission on the Promotion and Protection of Human Rights drafted its "Norms on the Responsibilities of Transnational Corporations and Other Business Enterprises with Regard to Human Rights" (Brownlie and Goodwin-Gill 2006, 268–74). These Norms included the preambular statement that "transnational corporations and other business enterprises, as organs of society, are . . . responsible for promoting and securing the human rights set forth in the Universal Declaration of Human Rights." The Norms enlarged the list of TNC human rights obligations mentioned in the Global Compact. In particular, they added security of persons, safe working conditions, and an adequate standard of living to the principles endorsed by the Compact, but like the ILO Declaration of Fundamental Principles and the Compact, they did not mention the right to strike. By the time of the writing of this book, the Norms had not been further entrenched in the UN legal system.

In February 2007, however, the UN Secretary-General's special representative on business and human rights, Professor John Ruggie, submitted a report to the UN General Assembly arguing that corporations had human rights responsibilities. Ruggie contended that there was "an expanding web of potential corporate responsibility for international crimes" (2007, par. 22). These crimes could include complicity in human rights violations committed by individuals in the employ of TNCs, such as violations of the right to life committed by TNC security forces. Thus, the UN promotes the view that TNCs and other businesses must become part of the international governance regime that protects human rights. Yet this legal regime of corporate responsibility for human rights is still weak at best and varies greatly by region and country (Ruggie 2007, pars. 33–44).

Along with these new international normative changes, in the past two decades some TNCs have begun to pay more attention to their effects on human rights and have adopted voluntary codes of human rights conduct, often called corporate social responsibility (CSR) codes. Determining the exact number of such codes is impossible, but by August 2008 at least 111 companies had human rights policies specifically referring to the UDHR (Business and Human Rights Resource Centre 2008). Notably, these codes of conduct rarely stipulated a fair wage for employees (Forsythe 2006, 240–41), despite the inclusion in the 2003 Norms of an adequate standard of living; European firms were more likely than North American to accept this obligation (Ruggie 2007, par. 67). Moreover, certain types of corporations more readily adopted human rights standards than others. For example, producers of sportswear, who were susceptible to boycotts by student consumers, protected themselves by introducing CSR codes.

Self-interest was often the underlying reason for the new corporate regard for human rights. Some corporations feared risking their reputations with a poor human rights record. Fewer consumers will buy from and fewer people will work for corporations that are believed to violate human rights (Gunderson 2006, 86). Similarly, ethical investors investigate corporations' human rights performance before deciding where they will invest their funds (Brysk 2005, 61–87); in 2008 one of every nine investment dollars under professional management in the United States involved some element of social responsibility (*Economist* 2008b, 4). The corporate world also suffered from a severe drop in public trust after major scandals among large U.S. companies in the early 2000s (Davies 2003, 307). Thus, forward-looking corporations, such as those in the international mining sector, incorporated human rights and environmental impact assessments into their investment decisions, in principle if not always in practice (Dashwood 2007). Socially responsible self-regulation became increasingly common in the 2000s, following the lead of the Kimberley Accord, which was devised to prohibit the sale of conflict diamonds from regions of Africa engaged in civil wars (Global Witness 2006). Given corporations' self-interest, a skeptic might regard this new social responsibility as simply an aspect of risk management (*Economist* 2008b, 12). Often CSR policies are introduced to garner good publicity, with public relations firms hired to promote companies' images (Stiglitz 2006, 199). Moreover, new TNCs not based in the democratic West may adopt CSR codes for purely self-serving reasons, avoiding any real accountability; for example, Chinese corporations are already adept at bribing CSR monitors or keeping double sets of books (Prieto-Carron et al. 2006, 982).

The actual impact of CSR policies to date is unknown; scholars suggest that assessment tools measure companies' compliance with their own CSR procedural rules, rather than the impact of those policies on society at large, an effect that may be too complicated to assess (Blowfield 2007, 693). The *Economist* argues that in any case the social responsibility of corporations is to make profits, thus contributing to economic growth and employment. For example, it cites a joint assessment by Oxfam, a development NGO, and Unilever, a TNC, of Unilever's activities in Indonesia in 2004–5, which found that Unilever "supported the equivalent of 300,000 full-time jobs . . . created a total value of at least $630m and contributed $130m a year in taxes to the Indonesian government" (*Economist* 2008b, 8).

In the final analysis, states are still responsible for the human rights behavior of TNCs, all of which have headquarters in one state or another.

States already possess plenty of tools to control TNCs' behavior. Governments could, for example, put human rights conditions on export credit loans or insist on human rights clauses when they negotiate trade or investment agreements with other governments. Rather than regulate TNCs directly, new international treaties could be written to oblige states to regulate the human rights behavior of TNCs based within their borders (Gibney 2008). Laws could be enacted enabling individuals harmed by a TNC to sue it in its home country, under international rules that would not give the TNC a "home court" advantage (Stiglitz 2006, 205– 7); such laws could also include provisions for global class action suits. Much room exists for regulation of TNCs within the present international human rights regime.

HUMAN RIGHTS OBLIGATIONS
OF INTERNATIONAL ORGANIZATIONS

The evolving interest in legal human rights obligations of TNCs affects policies of the IOs that regulate the global economy. By the late 1990s, international financial institutions (IFIs) were displaying more concern with the social dimensions of structural adjustment programs (SAPs). They were also including what might be considered human rights conditionality in their loan agreements, although this conditionality was couched in more neutral language of good governance, accountability, and the rule of law (Forsythe 1997, 339). Furthermore, in 1993 the World Bank (WB) introduced Inspection Panels composed of independent experts to whom citizens of less developed countries were permitted to complain about WB development policies (Fox 2002).

These small steps did not satisfy those who were concerned about WB accountability. The Inspection Panel is permitted to comment on WB procedures and recommend reforms but not to monitor what the WB does to implement those recommendations. One practice that particularly concerns WB critics is forcible displacement of people in order to build dams or complete other WB projects; at least two million people were so displaced by 2002 (Horta 2002, 237). Officially, the WB is supposed to ensure that displaced people are as well off or better off after being moved as they were before (Horta 2002, 237), but they are often much worse off. Another concern is the WB's claim that a prohibition on interference in the political affairs of a state means it is not permitted to take into account civil and political human rights when it makes lending decisions. Thus, critics note, it lends money to overtly authoritarian or brutal regimes. For example, the WB helped finance the Chad-Cameroon oil pipeline, even though the Chadian government used $4.5 million of its first payment from the WB to purchase arms for use against rebels (Clark 2002, 210 n.17).

Critics also argue that the WB is not accountable either to governments or to citizens who suffer because of its advice. Some journalists have suggested that the WB advised Malawi to end subsidies to farmers for fertilizers, and that this was one cause of famine in Malawi in 2002. According to these accounts, in 2007 Malawi decided, against WB advice, to reintroduce the subsidies. The result was an increase in production of maize (corn), Malawi's staple food, so great that Malawi began to export it, whereas previously it had relied on imports from the World Food Program (Masina 2008). In response to these accusations, the WB said that it supported the Malawian government's programs to subsidize fertilizer but suggested targeting recipients to make sure that the private market in fertilizers was not undermined; moreover, it contributed $30 million in 2005 to the targeted fertilizer subsidy program (World Bank 2008c). This suggests a higher level of cooperation with local government officials by the WB than many critics concede.

The WB also maintains that it is prohibited from taking civil and political rights into account in its policymaking by article 4, section 10 of its Articles of Agreement, which states that "only economic considerations shall be relevant" to its decisions (Horta 2002, 229), leaving "political" matters such as civil and political rights under states' sovereign control. Clapham argues that the prohibition on WB interference in the internal affairs of a state was meant to protect national sovereignty but was not meant to allow "general impunity from human rights accountability" (2006, 144). In 1998 the WB claimed that, in its view, attaining human rights was a central goal of development and the human dignity of the poorest was one of the foundations of its approach to development. Nevertheless, as of 2006 it had not instituted concrete measures to assess its impact on human rights (Clapham 2006, 154–55).

Some scholars contend that even if the IMF's and WB's own particular mandates do not include human rights, both must follow general international customary law, including human rights law. Their relationship to the UN means they are bound by the human rights obligations of the UN Charter, including the obligation to take steps to ensure that all individuals enjoy their economic, social, and cultural rights (Lindroos 2006; Fitzpatrick 2002). "The guiding principle should be that the international community is subject to human rights obligations similar to those of States. Thus, if a particular action by a national government would be viewed as a human rights violation, then a similar action by, say, the World Bank should be viewed as a human rights violation" (Kent 2005b).

In response, the IMF argues that its contributions to monetary stability, international exchange rate stability, and growth in international trade are significant contributions to economic human rights. Trade liberalization promotes economic growth, which normally improves the employment prospects and incomes of the poor. The IMF has stressed the central role of poverty reduction since 1999 and encourages countries that apply to it for funds to implement Poverty Reduction Strategies. Contrary to critics' views that the IMF advocates cuts in state expenditures on health or education, the IMF encourages governments to protect social expenditures; it points to data showing that countries with IMF-supported programs from 1985 to 1999 showed modest increases in social expenditures, resulting in improvements in several key indicators of citizens' well-being, such as reduced rates of infant and child mortality. Finally, according to the IMF, one should not assume that prior to countries' adoption of IMF policies, their social services were well run. Often services were poor yet very costly to taxpayers (Leite 2001).

The IMF's defense of its policies should be taken seriously. Poorly functioning economies in which governments overspend on inefficient or corruptly run social services will not effectively fulfill citizens' economic human rights. In the early twenty-first century, the IMF also began to take its explicit human rights obligations more seriously. A

2001 opinion by the IMF general counsel said that the IMF must consider the human rights implications of its recommended policies; it was not obliged to provide human rights but it was obliged not to violate them (Clapham 2006, 146).

Critics of IFIs also target the World Trade Organization (WTO), claiming that it privileges the interests of rich countries over poor. For example, although formally all states have equal status at the WTO, informally large states make private decisions among themselves before negotiating openly with all other states (Evans 2001, 97). Critics further argue that when the WTO was established, it should have incorporated a social clause to protect workers and consumers adversely affected by international trade. Clapham contends that insofar as the WTO or its dispute settlement mechanism acts as an independent body, it is bound by international human rights customary law just like any other organ of society (2006, 161–65).

The WTO's defenders maintain, to the contrary, that human rights obligations should not be imposed on it, as its function is merely to promote consensus among states so that freer trade will result (Jones 2004; Bhagwati 2004). The WTO is actually a fairly small agency with a very small budget (Legrain 2002, 178–79), and its officials have no independent decision-making power; they merely facilitate agreements among independent states. These agreements, defenders of the WTO argue, introduce stability and predictability into the world trade system and undermine the power of sectoral lobbies to deflect states from their legal commitments to free trade (Legrain 2002, 180–81). For example, in 2001 President George W. Bush was forced to withdraw a protective tariff against imported steel after a WTO ruling (Isbister 2006, 222). Freer trade benefits everyone, in the view of the WTO's defenders, because it stimulates national growth and employment; thus, it indirectly promotes economic human rights. Moreover, while a social clause to protect workers' rights was considered when the WTO was created, many less developed countries objected to it. They believed the social clause was a protectionist measure by the developed countries that would increase wages and other costs of production in poor countries, reducing their export competitiveness (Steinhardt 2005, 210).

Nevertheless, it appears that concern with human rights is slowly seeping into the WTO as trade negotiators introduce human rights standards, especially ILO minimum labor standards. Some ILO members have used applications from countries such as Vietnam and El Salvador to express dissatisfaction with the treatment of workers in EPZs. The WTO already permits signatory states to discriminate against products made by prison labor, and some scholars argue that this exception could also be applied to forced labor or child labor. Member states of the WTO are evidently paying more attention to their obligations under international law to uphold human rights standards (Aaronson 2007).

Despite their protests that they are not mandated to protect human rights, therefore, IOs already adhere to some human rights standards. Neither slavery nor genocide is permitted, for example, regardless of how useful they might hypothetically be to increasing national wealth. Some human rights prohibitions are so taken for granted that those who discuss the obligations of IOs might not even be aware that they are human rights principles, yet they suggest that it is possible for IOs to adopt additional human rights obligations. The inchoate application of international human rights law to IOs in the early twenty-first century may be strengthened in the future by more formalized legal obligations, better procedures for measuring the human rights impact of IOs' various policies, and greater commitment of member states not only to the human rights of their own citizens but also to the human rights of the citizens of other states.

At the moment, though, structural problems limit IOs' capacity to protect human rights. One such problem is a severe administrative deficit, especially in the area of accountability. IOs introduce, implement, and evaluate policies on their own terms without outside financial accounting. Real accountability requires standards and the potential for sanctions (Chesterman 2008, 43), but such sanctions cannot apply to the IFIs until they are also subject to political accountability. Despite the IFIs' insistence on accountability and transparency from the governments with whom they deal, their own internal discussion and decisions are often masked in secrecy (de Senarclens 2003, 154–55).

Defenders of IFIs point out that they are accountable to their international boards of directors, individual members of which represent their own governments; in the case of democracies, at least, these governments in turn represent their own people. However, while citizens of rich democracies are rarely affected by IFI policies, citizens of poor, often undemocratic countries are frequently affected yet have little, if any, say in drafting them. In 2008 Africa, the Middle East, Latin America, and Asia (without China) collectively controlled only about 27.5 percent of the votes on the IMF Board of Directors (International Monetary Fund 2008). Thus, there is a severe democratic deficit, which suggests that "the people and the governments of developing states are not effectively involved in decisions affecting their lives" (McCorquodale and Fairbrother 1999, 746). Critics also argue that more mechanisms should be available for NGOs and individual citizens to have a direct say in IO policymaking; however, some note that NGOs in turn are neither fully accountable nor representative, and that the most prominent NGOs sometimes put forward the most extreme views (Chesterman 2008, 49).

NOT LEAPING FAR ENOUGH

Any assessment of how far human rights have leaped over time and space would have to conclude that so far they have come up short; TNCs and IOs are still very weakly bound by human rights norms. Since 1990 they have accepted some human rights responsibilities, but at least in the case of TNCs these responsibilities are still mainly voluntary, and often TNCs ignore or manipulate them in their own interests. While "capitalism is global in scope . . . the controls it faces at the global level are laughably weak" (Isbister 2006, 229). Individuals wanting protection of their human rights would still be better off going to their governments than to an IO for assistance. In the event that their government violated human rights, the best means to pressure it to change its policies would be via the national and international human rights social movement, not the formal organizations and rules of global governance.

7

CIVIL SOCIETY

Human rights have leapfrogged not only to new bearers of human rights obligations but also to new advocates for human rights. Increasingly, global governance responds to globalization from below, as citizens participate in developing rules for the global market economy and recommending the constraints and obligations they believe ought to be placed upon it. Citizens in places now being reached by the second great transformation are not in the same social position as those affected by the first. They need not wait 150 or 200 years before attaining their human rights. Indeed, globalization speeds up their access to the very idea of rights, thus presenting them with a new language with which to articulate their concerns.

CIVIL SOCIETY

I use the term "civil society" to refer to organizations of citizens below the level of, and independent of, the state that peacefully pursue collective social objectives. These include social movements and nongovernmental organizations (NGOs) whose objectives are to influence domestic governments, international organizations (IOs), and transnational corporations (TNCs). Global civil society consists of individuals, groups, and organizations physically located in different countries and regions, yet able to communicate with one another and organize as international pressure groups. This definition of civil society assumes that citizens' organizations are, indeed, civil—that is, that they are peaceful and do not engage in criminal activities (Brysk 2005, 125). Human rights NGOs (HRNGOs) are a particular subset of civil society. They are devoted to the promotion and protection of human rights, are "independent of both governmental and political groups that seek direct political power," and do not themselves seek political power (Wiseberg 1991, 529). By 1998 there were at least 325 international HRNGOs (Smith, Pagnucco, and Lopez 1998, 383).

Global social movements for human rights existed before globalization; for example, there was a global social movement against the slave trade in the late eighteenth and early nineteenth centuries. Since the transformation of the global communications network by electronic means, however, globalization has intensified and sped up civil society's capacity to organize. Through e-mail and the Internet, civil society actors have immediate access to knowledge, immediate capacity to criticize policy decisions by governments, IOs, and TNCs, and immediate capacity to interact with one another. Citizens are no longer mere consumers of information; they are generators of knowledge and debaters about social issues.

The civil society actors who now populate global public space possess an "ability to forge links with popular struggles at the most local level anywhere in the world" (Beetham 1998, 68). Citizens of oppressive regimes, such as in China, post information about human rights abuses on the Internet; as fast as their government shuts down one website and confiscates some computers, users of new computers create new websites. Human rights abuses are now subject to "cosmopolitan publicity" in a transnational public sphere (Bohman 1999, 506). Thus, globalization provides new and expanded space for civil society, especially HRNGOs and citizens' social movements.

A social movement can be defined as "a collection of formal organizations, informal networks, and unaffiliated individuals engaged in a more or less coherent struggle for change" (Meyer and Whittier 1994, 277). Sometimes social movements are very loosely organized or coordinated;

at other times, they are very well organized and coordinated, particularly through networks of NGOs. NGOs are relatively formal, bureaucratized organizations with a specific mandate or purpose. Members of social movements may support NGOs whose goals coincide with their own, but they may also engage in more loosely defined or controlled activities, such as demonstrating at meetings of the International Monetary Fund (IMF) or World Trade Organization (WTO). Together, these NGOs and social movements constitute transnational advocacy networks (Keck and Sikkink 1998) pushing simultaneously on local, national, and international fronts and using both formal and informal means to obtain their goals. These networks benefit not only from electronic communications but also from the ease of travel of the last thirty years. People from all parts of the globe meet face to face at international conferences of particular NGOs or at various NGO networking events. The line between social movement and NGOs blurs as such large gatherings reinforce less organized social movements.

THE GLOBAL HUMAN RIGHTS SOCIAL MOVEMENT

The single most important concern of globalization's critics (as well as many of its advocates) is poverty. It is very difficult, however, to organize social movements to eliminate poverty, given its entrenched nature and the fact that so many events, policies, and actors are implicated in causing it over a long time period and wide geographic area. It is not enough to blame international capitalism or globalization for poverty. Many political and social factors internal to nation-states contribute to it, not least whether or not the poor enjoy civil and political rights.

During the first great transformation, the most important anticapitalist civil society organizations were based on social class. Workers demonstrated for the right to vote and organized trade unions to protect their interests in the workplace, often forming alliances with communist, socialist, or social democratic political parties (Ishay 2004, 118–72). This, in turn, depended on state toleration of these political parties; left-wing political parties were persecuted not only in nondemocratic countries but also in democratic countries such as the United States (Goldstein 1987, 430–36).

Class action and organization is as necessary during the second great transformation as it was in the first. Transformation of the human rights situation of ordinary people must include a social movement for workers' rights. This is so even when all economic indicators are positive and when the rule of law and democracy seem "naturally" to evolve. Workers require specific protections of their rights from violations by both local and international governors and employers—hence the importance of the International Labor Organization's (ILO) core labor standards. Workers require these protections even more when economic indicators are negative and when the rule of law and democratic politics disappear.

Since the 1980s, some middle-income or developing countries have enjoyed national economic growth in part because they established export processing zones (EPZs). EPZs are industrial areas set up by national governments who offer foreign investors in these areas a variety of incentives, including low or no rents, tax exemptions for many years, and a guarantee that workers will not be permitted to form trade unions. The working conditions in some of these EPZs more closely resemble slavery than free labor, as the Canadian journalist and activist Naomi Klein found. Visiting a Philippine EPZ called Cavite in 1997, she discovered people obliged to work nineteen-hour shifts, some of them living in closely packed "dormitories" in former pigpens (2000, 208, 215). It was common in EPZs for employers to hire new workers and force them to labor on double shifts during peak demand for their goods, then lay them off when demand was slow, a process known as "hire and fire" (2000, 217). Klein's exposé demonstrates the need for all workers, everywhere and at all times, to enjoy the protection of trade unions. Free trade unions and the right to strike are key to workers' rights in industrial economies. Unregulated capitalism may improve national growth figures, but it often does so at the severe expenses of workers.

However, class action resembling the activities of labor unions in the nineteenth-century Western world may not be the only or even the most important type of social action necessary to control the adverse effects of capitalism in the twenty-first century. Labor unions are no longer a strong force in North America, although they still wield influence in some western European countries (Atleson 2006). Nor, in countries in which the global market affects rural agricultural producers as much as urban workers, are trade unions able to defend the interests of all whose livelihoods are undermined by globalization. Consumers as well as producers need protection in the global marketplace, and globalization's adverse environmental effects affect the entire world. Thus, trade unions are now only one type of NGO in a wide array of groups attempting to ameliorate various detrimental aspects of globalization.

The most effective social movements and NGOs critical of globalization tend to focus on specific abuses of economic human rights, especially by TNCs. In the 1970s, one of the first international social movements for economic rights (although not then defined as such) objected to Nestlé Corporation's campaign to persuade new mothers in the developing world to use infant formula, even if they could breastfeed. Many mothers could not afford the necessary amount of formula, so they watered down what they had, often using unsterilized water. An international consumer boycott persuaded Nestlé to change its marketing strategy (Keck and Sikkink 1998).

The success of international campaigns such as the Nestlé boycott depends on good organization and even on particular incidents that capture public attention (Bob 2002). For example, the world became aware of the environmental damage in southeast Nigeria caused by transnational oil companies only after the tragic hanging of the civil society leader Ken Saro-Wiwa in 1995, which generated much international media coverage (Skogly 1997; Welch 1995). However, consumer campaigns can backfire, as in the case of the Swiss grocery chain Migros, which in 1987 inserted a social clause into its contract with Del Monte to ensure that working conditions on the latter's Philippine pineapple farms were above average. The price of Del Monte's pineapples then rose, and some consumers reacted by buying cheaper pineapples produced by Del Monte's competitors, who may not have paid their workers above-average wages (Pangalangan 2002, 108).

Social movements are also more likely to succeed when ordinary citizens are touched by abuse of vulnerable groups, children in particular.

The Rugmark campaign of the 1990s told consumers whether rugs from Asia were made by child labor, exerting pressure for improved labor standards in Pakistan and Iran (Pangalangan 2002, 107). Consumer organizations sometimes use a "spotlight effect" to focus on specific abuses by specific firms (Spar 1998); for example, a consumer campaign during the 1990s persuaded Reebok to stop buying soccer balls from Pakistani subcontractors who used child labor. The cumulative effect of these consumer campaigns is strong, especially when the item under scrutiny is a discretionary product that consumers can do without.

The largest antiglobalization social movement is the one that targets global capitalism directly. Since 1999 demonstrations at major meetings of states, international financial institutions (IFIs), or business and other elite groups have been common. Demonstrators at the 1999 WTO meeting in Seattle shouted slogans such as "Hell no, WTO," reminiscent of the slogan of the 1970s campaign against the military draft during the Vietnam War, "Hell no, we won't go!" (Hertel 2005, 113). In 2001 demonstrators used a variety of tactics, from peaceful demonstrations to street theatre to violence against property, to protest the Summit of the Americas, a meeting of American states being held in Quebec City (Drainville 2005). One response by governments to such demonstrations has been to make the sites of these meetings increasingly more remote (Smith 2009). Governments and IOs also treat demonstrators as security risks rather than as people exercising their democratic right to freedom of expression. In Genoa in 2001 a paramilitary police officer killed a demonstrator protesting the G8 summit, a meeting of the world's seven leading industrial powers plus Russia.

The World Social Forum (WSF), a mass movement encompassing tens of thousands of activists critical of globalization, began meeting at Porto Alegre, Brazil, in 2001; by 2006 it was drawing one hundred fifty thousand participants at various locations, including Mumbai, India, in 2004. The WSF's purpose is to teach networks of activists the skills necessary for global-level advocacy (Smith 2006a). Its slogan, "another world is possible" (Smith 2006b, 879), advocates transformation rather than mere reformation of the global market. Without specific targets, however, and without a clear agenda to remedy specific abuses (Teivainen

2002; Smith 2004), the WSF and similar mass movements are unlikely to be effective, except to indicate activists' dissatisfaction with global capitalism. More targeted social movements are more successful, such as the movement to pursue justice for people displaced from their farms and villages by government programs to build large dams (Goulet 2005).

Paralleling the international social movement against globalization, the late twentieth and early twenty-first centuries witnessed unprecedented attention to environmental degradation. Global warming and environmental damage appear in large part to be a consequence of the industrialization of new parts of the globe; in 2007 an intergovernmental scientific panel concluded that human activities "very likely" were a major cause of climate change (Intergovernmental Panel on Climate Change 2007). Contributing to environmental damage was the "consume and waste" nature of advanced capitalist societies, which paid insufficient attention to their responsibilities to future generations (Stephens and Bullock 2004, 143). Environmental activists joined with human rights activists to preserve the environment and citizens' rights to enjoy it.

On the other side of the social spectrum from those adversely affected by global capitalism, some leaders of the social movement against poverty are celebrities like rock stars Bob Geldof and Bono and movie star Angelina Jolie. These pop culture figures are often more successful in mobilizing younger people for human rights than more established and formal NGOs such as Amnesty International (AI). With worldwide coverage of their concerts made possible by the advanced communications of the twenty-first century, popular singers reach hundreds of millions of young people, as during the 2005–6 Make Poverty History campaign, meant to pressure the G8 at its 2006 meeting. Bono and Geldof also began to infiltrate the corridors of power, attending the annual World Economic Forum meetings in Davos, Switzerland, formerly reserved only for politicians and corporate chief executive officers (Cooper 2008).

Bono and Geldof use the politics of shame and adverse publicity to persuade political and corporate leaders to devote more resources to the alleviation of global debt and poverty. They also lead consumer campaigns like the Red Campaign begun in 2006, in which major consumer chains such as the Gap donate a portion of profits from designated products to the anti-HIV/AIDS campaign in Africa. Celebrity diplomacy is complemented by the emergence of celebrity economists, including Jeffrey Sachs, who leverage their access to politicians, film stars, and corporate donors to find financing for their proposed solutions to global poverty (Sachs 2005). These new celebrity endeavors are complemented in turn by renewed attention to global philanthropy. For example, Bill Gates, the founder of Microsoft, and his wife, Melinda, set up the Gates Foundation to promote global health, persuading billionaire Warren Buffett to join them.

HUMAN RIGHTS NONGOVERNMENTAL ORGANIZATIONS

Social movements and HRNGOs often work in concert. HRNGOs can also be seen as part of global governance, insofar as they insert private citizen organizations into discussions of norms, rules, and institutional responsibilities of states and IOs. Indeed, civil society organizations such as the antipoverty group Oxfam are themselves now global institutions (Giddens 2003, xxv).

As of 2007, approximately three thousand NGOs, including HRNGOs, enjoyed formal consultative status at various UN agencies; others were invited to participate at UN meetings and consultations. The UN Committee on NGOs, comprised of nineteen member states, decided which NGOs were to be granted consultative status. However, its members sometimes permitted political matters to influence their decisions; for example, the NGO Human Rights in China was denied accreditation at the World Summit on the Information Society in Tunis in 2007. Furthermore, many government-organized NGOs (GONGOs) were accredited at the UN, and these frequently supported their governments' positions (Bloem, Attia, and Dam 2008).

Despite this politicization, formal consultative status permits HRNGOs to offer advice to the various UN organs concerned with human rights. HRNGOs also frequently organize side-conferences to formal UN meetings, as they did at the 1993 World Conference on Human Rights in Vienna. Some NGOs have acquired the diplomatic skills necessary to engage with policymakers face to face; the Montreal International Forum, an NGO that attended G8 meetings from 2002 to 2006, gradually accumulated enough credibility for various official participants to engage with it (Martin 2008). Individual NGO actors have formed personal relationships with individual officials. Thus, Jo Marie Griesgraber, an anti-debt activist, was able to organize a small group to suggest reforms in accountability and transparency at the IMF, which were eventually adopted (Griesgraber 2008). Most HRNGOs, however, do not have as close links with the agencies of global governance as these examples suggest.

HRNGOs often incur criticism for focusing too much on civil and political rather than economic rights. When the global human rights social movement began, most major HRNGOs, such as AI and Human Rights Watch (HRW), did focus on civil and political rights, especially torture, extrajudicial execution, and disappearances (Baehr 1994; Clark 2001). Yet in the late twentieth and early twenty-first centuries, many HRNGOs introduced economic human rights into their mandates. AI changed its mandate in 2002 to encompass all human rights and began campaigns on matters such as corporate human rights responsibility (Baehr 2003). HRW decided that it could not focus on failures to fulfill economic human rights but could report on specific violations, particularly if they were consequences of arbitrary or discriminatory judgments by states (Roth 2004).

Some of the most influential HRNGOs are professional organizations. The medical organization Doctors without Borders, established in 1971, has stepped beyond its original disinterested treatment of all who need medical attention to criticism of governments and advocacy of policy change (Doctors Without Borders/Médecins Sans Frontières 2009). Since their inceptions, organizations such as Lawyers for Human Rights, founded in 1979, and Reporters Without Borders, founded in 1985, have had more explicit political agendas, criticizing governments for abusing civil and political rights, freedom of expression, and the rule of law. While their agendas do not explicitly critique globalization, these professional organizations protect civil society actors who engage in such critiques. Equally important are the many faith-based groups concerned with development and economic human rights. These include not only many Christian groups, often the lineal descendants of missionaries, but other faith-based organizations like the Agha Khan Foundation, established by the leader of the world's Shia Imami Ismaili Muslims.

While some NGOs are dedicated to specific human rights, others represent particular interest groups and overlap with or concretize wider social movements that include individuals not affiliated with any NGOs. The feminist movement was solidly international as of the 1980s; women from all over the world met at the official UN conferences on women's rights held in Mexico City, Copenhagen, Nairobi, and Beijing in 1975, 1980, 1985, and 1995, respectively (Chen 1996; Stamatopoulou 1995). Their common interests included defense of female workers' rights in countries experiencing rapid transnational investment and advocacy for women driven into poverty or whose poverty deepened as a result of structural adjustment policies.

Women were not the only marginalized people to organize. In 1975 the World Council of Indigenous Peoples was formed. Indigenous peoples living around the North Pole in Canada, Alaska, Russia, and Greenland held the first Circumpolar Conference in 1977. One of the NGOs assisting them was Survival International, founded in 1969 to campaign for the rights of tribal peoples. In 2007 the combined efforts of these social movements and NGOs led the United Nations General Assembly to adopt the Declaration on the Rights of Indigenous Peoples. This Declaration includes "the right . . . to the improvement of their [indigenous peoples'] economic . . . conditions, including . . . education, employment . . . housing, sanitation, health and social security" (United Nations General Assembly 2007, article 21, 1), thus entrenching economic human rights as a key aspect of indigenous rights.

HRNGOs often linked the developed and nondeveloped parts of the globe, though such coalitions revealed tensions among the different civil society players from the global north and south—that is, the developed and less developed regions. Jubilee 2000, an NGO that campaigned successfully for debt relief for poor countries, united civil society organizations in more than seventy countries. Northern members of Jubilee commanded more financial and organizational resources than southern members, and there were disagreements about whether to work with or against national governments, eventually resulting in some southern organizations forming a separate Jubilee South (Buxton 2004).

Nevertheless, one of the advantages of north-south civil society alliances is "boomeranging." Unable in some cases to directly affect their own governments' policies, some southern NGOs pressure northern governments through their northern NGO allies; this pressure boomerangs back onto the southern governments as northern governments respond to their own citizens' concerns about human rights conditions within the southern country (Keck and Sikkink 1998, 13). Sometimes, however, southern NGOs disagree with northern NGOs' aims or tactics. In the 1990s, a campaign in the United States against child labor in the Bangladeshi garment industry resulted in tens of thousands of children losing their jobs, without alternate means of support for themselves or their families. Bangladeshi feminist groups argued that the layoffs of children violated their economic rights to subsistence and work; they blocked the campaign until provisions were made to provide the laid-off children with education and their families with alternate sources of income (Hertel 2006, 31–54).

These examples point to more general problems in the international human rights movement. Often southern HRNGOs are financed in whole or part by northern charities, such as the Rockefeller or Ford foundations, whose agendas then become the agendas of the HRNGOs whom they finance. Such funding can have a corrosive effect on HRNGO independence and provoke resentment, especially when HRNGO personnel receive much better pay, housing, and transportation than that of co-nationals working in other sectors (Dicklitch 1998; Englund 2006). Additionally, northern governments sometimes fund southern HRNGOs, which must then work through the bureaucratic hurdles of learning to write grant proposals and keeping financial records according to northern standards. Funding from northern governments might also be viewed as overly politicized.

Despite all these criticisms, civil society by the twenty-first century was an important part of global governance. The activities of HRNGOs and the social movement critical of globalization together increased the likelihood that those adversely affected by globalization could fight for their human rights. Some significant policy changes resulted from HRNGO campaigns. Jubilee successfully pressured the G8 countries for debt relief (Buxton 2004). The British NGO Global Witness and the Canadian NGO Partnership Africa Canada led a campaign against conflict diamonds that resulted in the Kimberley Accord, an agreement among producers and purchasers not to trade in diamonds illegally exported from conflict zones such as Sierra Leone and the Congo (Smillie 2004). HRNGOs also successfully worked with less developed countries to take advantage of a WTO exemption to intellectual property rights that allowed them to import generic drugs to treat HIV/AIDS (He and Murphy 2007). All of these were narrowly targeted campaigns, however. Diffuse social movements that seek to overhaul the entire system of global trade—the WSF, for instance—have had far less marked success.

GLOBAL GOVERNANCE AND CIVIL SOCIETY

Figure 7.1 shows the many aspects of the global order that now affect the spread of human rights. The right-hand side presents the simplified view of how universal human rights are created: the development of markets expands national wealth, in turn helping to create a larger middle class that demands rule of law, a democratic political system, and democratic accountability. All of these buttress the evolving conception of universal human rights, but human rights are realized in practice only when other normative changes, governance innovations, and social movements are involved. On the left-hand side, the global normative order (the ideology of human rights) supports the global human rights regime, one aspect of global governance. Global governance requires IOs, including particular branches of the UN, to be preoccupied with human rights; it also pressures IOs such as IFIs to incorporate human rights into their mandates. The global media spreads knowledge of the human rights regime and publicizes violations of human rights. From below, global civil society and the global human rights social movement (including the social movement to reform globalization) push for human rights. Traditional NGOs, especially trade unions, continue to participate

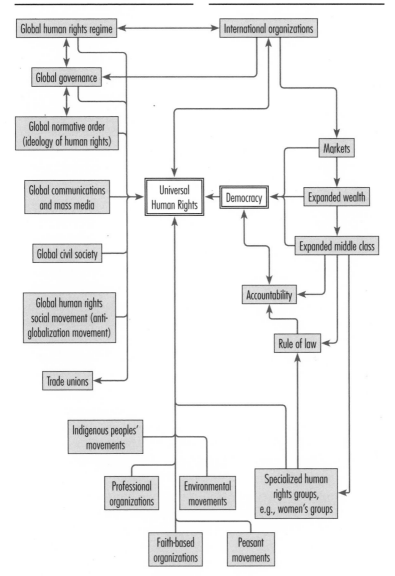

Figure 7.1   Social Action and Human Rights

in the anticapitalist struggle, joined by environmentalists, faith-based groups, and professional organizations. Specialized interest groups such as indigenous peoples', peasants', and feminist organizations likewise join the struggle.

Thus, globalization speeds up not only capitalist expansion but also resistance to capitalism. It is increasingly difficult for authoritarian states or self-interested TNCs to prevent citizens from obtaining information about violations of economic human rights. As global communication erodes geographical remoteness, the universal principle of human rights becomes one upon which local actors can base their demands for justice. Global human rights, anticapitalist, and antiglobalization groups form a social movement that demands accountability for the damage that globalization can cause.

This does not mean, however, that all civil society organizations agree on all matters. Moreover, even if HRNGOs or members of the social movement to reform globalization have altruistic motives, their analysis is not always correct. In particular, if HRNGO or social movement leaders persist in arguing that free trade is detrimental to the interests of the poor when economic data shows that free trade raises both national and individual incomes in countries that globalize, they may do more harm than good.

Serious attempts to protect economic human rights require that HRNGO and social movement leaders, as well as academic critics of globalization, understand economics. In her exposé of working conditions in EPZs, for example, Klein criticizes a seemingly heartless statement by the Nobel Prize–winning (in 2008) economist Paul Krugman, who argued, "The overwhelming mainstream view among economists is that the growth of this kind of employment [in EPZs] is tremendous good news for the world's poor" (Klein 2000, 228). The good news was both economic growth for entire countries or regions and higher incomes than would otherwise have been possible for many EPZ workers, in jobs that often prevented their having to take up alternative "employment" as garbage pickers or sex workers. The bad news was the terrible working conditions, sometimes including below-subsistence wages, often endured by these workers. These contradictions ought to be reconciled, but the way to do so is by allowing workers their rights, not by rejecting the

market economy. Pressure on exporting governments to protect workers' rights frequently does result in laws that generate improvements on
the factory floor (Greenhill, Mosley, and Prakash 2008); HRNGOs that
generate such pressure are more effective than critics who advocate a
simple ban on EPZs.

HRNGOs focus not only on TNCs but also on the IFIs that make
many of the decisions affecting workers and the poor. Defenders of IFIs
sometimes question the right of unelected NGOs to claim to represent
citizens' interests; elected officials, they say, are the appropriate people to
make decisions about the world economy (Legrain 2002, 204). In this
view, democratically elected officials appoint representatives to act on
their behalf and on their instructions in IOs. When these representatives vote in the IMF, the WB, or the WTO for liberalized world trade,
they presumably have the best interests of the poor at heart, as much as
or more than social movements and HRNGOs that wish to reform globalization. IOs are thus directed by representatives of sovereign governments—still the institutions with the most power to influence economic
policy and the most legitimacy to do so. In reply, however, one can argue
that democracies require dissent; in the absence of more formalized
means to express dissent within IOs, NGOs are the most legitimate and
effective organizations to bring the concerns of those adversely affected
by globalization to the table (Price 2003, 591–92). Furthermore, TNCs
by definition are not accountable, except to shareholders; without NGO
pressure, they might well not adopt even a pretense of concern for consumers, the environment, or the wider public.

Nevertheless, NGOs are not always correct in their analysis. Larry
Summers, secretary of the U.S. Treasury under President Bill Clinton
and later an economic advisor to President Barack Obama, said in 2001
that "a large number of things those [nongovernmental] organizations
say are not true and if they were acted on would be inimical to the goal
of reducing poverty around the world" (Buxton 2004, 71). An example of
such problematic analysis occurred at the Freedom from Want session of
the Millenium+5 Summit, convened in 2005 to discuss progress toward
the Millennium Development Goals (MDGs) declared by the UN in
2000. The MDGs are a set of eight development goals to be achieved by

2015, such as halving the 1990 rates of world poverty and hunger (Isbister 2006, 185). NGO participants at the session criticized "the prevailing approach to development that is centered on markets and not on human beings" (Bloem, Attia, and Dam 2008, 62). This is a standard antiglobalization critique that does not acknowledge that human beings participate in markets as producers, distributors, and consumers. NGO participants also criticized the MDGs for "relying on the discredited notion that economic growth can reduce poverty" (Bloem, Attia, and Dam 2008, 62). This notion is not discredited; there is much evidence for it. Finally, some NGOs argued that "economic growth is not a solution in itself because the origin of poverty lies in income distribution" (Bloem, Attia, and Dam 2008, 63). Unequal distribution of income is indeed one cause of poverty, but simple lack of national wealth is another.

Rejecting mainstream economists' arguments about the causes of poverty and wealth and about the advantages of market economies may be emotionally satisfying. Rejection, however, can increase the likelihood of poverty, as it did in the communist economies of the twentieth century. While civil society's attempts to protect the poor are important checks on pure market forces, the poor are better served if HRNGOs and social movements seriously engage with those who argue for market economies, rather than ignoring them. On the other hand, reform often occurs when those in power engage with moderates in an attempt to stave off criticisms by radicals. Street demonstrations against the institutions of world capitalist power are a means to force those who might otherwise entirely ignore the world's poor to think again.

THE POLITICS OF RESENTMENT

CONTRADICTORY EFFECTS OF THE GREAT TRANSFORMATIONS

The preceding two chapters suggest that one might be cautiously optimistic about human rights leapfrogging. Although the early twenty-first century was a time of world insecurity caused in part by globalization, both the human rights regime and civil society activism demonstrated some limited capacity to control those aspects of globalization that were more harmful than beneficial. Yet the damage caused by, or perceived to have been caused by, globalization may already be so great that slow, steady progress toward protection of human rights—civil and political as well as economic—will not occur everywhere in the world. Many millions of individuals may feel so besieged by the cultural, economic, and political influences of capitalism and democracy—both, to them, emanations of "Western" dominance over their lives—that they turn to a politics of resentment. This resentment may check, or even reverse, some of the positive effects of globalization as some areas of the world resort to culturalist assertions of autonomy from the West, or even to quasi-fascist social movements. Thus, the global human rights movement may well leap backward, not forward. In the early twenty-first century, parts of the Muslim world seemed most likely to experience such backward leaps, although resentment was not absent from other areas, such as authoritarian China.

Polanyi wrote about the "double movement" of the first great transformation, both toward and away from the self-regulating market system that he argued was the ideological aim of nineteenth-century economists—just as free market globalization was thought to be the ideological aim of neoliberal economists in the late twentieth century. Polanyi believed that as the market expanded it was met by counter movements that ultimately undermined it (1944, 130). Part of the reaction against the market consisted of such self-protective social movements as trade unionism. Another part, however, consisted of complete reaction against the social changes of the modern, capitalist era, culminating in fascism. Describing early to mid-twentieth-century reactions against modernity and capitalism, Polanyi noted "the spread of irrationalistic philosophies, racialist esthetics, anticapitalist demagogy, heterodox currency views, criticism of the [democratic] party system, widespread disparagement of the 'regime,' or whatever was the name given to the existing democratic setup" (1944, 238).

Some of these reactions are occurring again in the twenty-first century as people negatively affected by globalization resist it. The rapidity and confusion of social change and the consequent economic insecurity that they suffer intensify the reaction against the West, especially the United States. Many are particularly angry about the spread of "Western"—often thought to be American—values and customs, especially individualism, equality of men and women, and sexual freedom, most recently symbolized by the struggle for gay and lesbian rights. As Bilahari Kausikan, a Singaporean diplomat, argued about democracy, "The Western approach is ideological, not empirical. The West needs its myths; missionary zeal to whip the heathen along the path of righteousness and remake the world in its own image is deeply engrained in Western (especially American) political culture" (1993, 33). His comment easily applies to human rights as well as to democracy. The dilemma, then, is to how promote the beneficial aspects of globalization, and the democracy and human rights sometimes connected to it, while not uprooting societies wholesale from their familiar cultures, ways of belonging, and understandings of the world.

Benjamin Barber (1995) worried that globalization would result in "Jihad vs. McWorld." "Jihad" symbolizes a cultural reaction against

Western social norms—a retreat into conservative religious doctrines and cultural forms—while "McWorld" symbolizes the complete commercialization of the world and the transformation of all values into degraded materialism. Both McWorld and Jihad undermine democracy, according to Barber. McWorld is characterized by the "economic totalism of unleashed market economies [that] . . . subordinate politics, society and culture to the demands of an overarching market" (1995, 295); Jihad is the antidemocratic reaction to that market. Antimarket social movements may increase their influence in the twenty-first century and reject human rights as well. Some observers already regard the universal human rights regime as hypocritical, viewing those Western activists who offer their well-meaning assistance to the victims of globalization as the sisters and brothers of those who exploit them. Those who blame Westerners for the wrenching social and economic changes they are now experiencing frequently join with authoritarian governments to suppress the human rights movement, claiming it is an inauthentic, nonindigenous, Western cultural imposition.

The politics of resentment against the West is particularly directed against the United States. In a 2005 poll, residents of five predominantly Muslim Middle Eastern countries characterized Americans as "greedy, violent, rude and immoral" (Kohut and Wike 2008). In a 2007 poll conducted in forty-seven countries, the majority of Muslims as well as other non-Westerners admired U.S. ideas about science but were divided over U.S. ideas about business and democracy. In several countries more than 50 percent of those polled—and in some countries over 80 percent—said they disliked American music, movies, and television (Pew Global Attitudes Project 2007, 100–103). For many, the United States represents a world of social change and confusion, and Americans appear "rootless, cosmopolitan, superficial, trivial, materialistic" (Buruma and Margalit 2004, 8).

Anti-Americanism increased dramatically after the attacks on the World Trade Center and Pentagon on September 11, 2001, despite a short upsurge of support for the United States immediately following the attack. Hollander describes anti-Americanism as "an unfocused and largely irrational, often visceral aversion toward the United States, its government, domestic institutions, foreign policies, prevailing values, culture, and people. It appears to be born out of a scapegoating impulse fueled by a wide variety of frustrations and grievances" (1995, 334–35). This description, written before 9/11, does not take into account the anger many people felt toward the United States after it began to arrest, incarcerate, and torture terrorism suspects and after it attacked Iraq in 2003.

Political resentment has forced some Americans to look at themselves in a new light. As Wallerstein argues, "The United States has always defined itself . . . by the yardstick of the world. We are better; we were better; we shall be better. . . . we are more civilized than the rest of the world. . . . We represent the highest aspirations of everyone, not merely Americans. We are the leader of the free world, because we are the freest country in the world, and others look to us for leadership" (2001, 1, 7). It is no longer the case, if it ever was, that the United States represents everyone's highest aspirations; rather, for many people it now represents everything that is evil about the West and globalization. They assume that the United States has no interest in the needs or aspirations of anyone other than Americans (Pew Global Attitudes Project 2007, 97).

Given the distrust of the United States and the Western world, and political manifestations of this distrust, perhaps it is best to leave the non-Western world and non-Western governments to cope as best they can with the intensified social changes that result from globalization. Alternately, we can try to understand the contradictory and negative aspects of globalization in order to predict what new human rights problems are likely to emerge and how to manage them. Four characteristics of globalization seem to particularly intensify the politics of resentment: the declining autonomy of the nation-state, the intensified transnational class structure, changing aspects of social life, and weakened national cultural autonomy.

POLITICAL AND SOCIAL CHANGES EXACERBATING RESENTMENT

The state occupies a contradictory role in the creation of a world in which human rights are universal. It is both the chief vehicle for protecting its citizens' human rights and the chief perpetrator of human rights abuses within its own territory. The international human rights regime lacks enforcement powers, so citizens still rely on their own states to protect their human rights. Yet globalization predicts states' declining authority as they relinquish aspects of their sovereignty to global trade and global rules. On the other hand, more and more states are adopting global norms of democracy and human rights; although they relinquish sovereignty, their commitment to their citizens' rights improves. In some countries, the optimistic model discussed in chapter 4 seems to be becoming a reality.

This global spread of democracy suggests the possibility of global liberal politics. Contemporary liberal political regimes are characterized by individual freedom, choice, and tolerance of difference. Freedom of speech is a key aspect of liberalism; combined with the new technology of global communications, it allows a global marketplace of ideas to accompany the global market in products. This liberal ideal is so attractive that wherever citizens are permitted to speak their minds, they demand that their national governments allow political freedom. Liberal democracy could become the political norm worldwide, validating Fukuyama's prediction of the "end of history," in the sense that just as there is now only one economic game in the globalized world—capitalism—so there is only one ideological game—liberalism. As Fukuyama put it, "The triumph of the West . . . is evident first of all in the total exhaustion of viable systematic alternatives to Western liberalism" (1989, 3).

However, if liberalism becomes the only legitimate political ideology, this could induce some states to reject human rights as an operative principle of government. Declining international legitimacy of nonliberal regimes could encourage culturalist resentment of the West and a retreat to societies based on illiberal beliefs, often rooted in religion. Many Muslims prefer the familiarity of their own community, with its emphasis on religious membership, to the harsh strangeness of the new global society. Members of other religions manifest the same reaction to liberal social values. In the United States, some conservative Christians object to certain manifestations of freedom of choice, such as women's and gay and lesbian rights.

Globalization also causes resentment by intensifying the transnational nature of class structure. Even in liberal democratic societies that no longer legally discriminate against racial or ethnic minorities, against women, or against other groups, social classes still exist; the rich and the comfortable middle classes are differentiated from the poor. In the international class structure, it seems, the poor are abandoned while the rich seek their fortunes on the global stage (Sassen 2007, 164–89). An international class of business owners and managers shares a common entrepreneurial culture that transcends the nation-states of which they are citizens or in which their firms and businesses are located. Many members of this international business class are migrants from the Third World to the First World (as they used to be known)—for example, from China or India to the United States. Their migration is supplemented by the migration of highly trained professionals, especially medical personnel.

Their skills, knowledge, and positions in transnational firms seem to remove these entrepreneurs and professionals from local settings, yet travel is now so easy and inexpensive that migration from one continent to another no longer means the end of ties to one's home country or extended family, as it did for migrants in the eighteenth, nineteenth, and early twentieth centuries. Well-off individuals may experience "postnational citizenship," legally holding double or even triple citizenship. This postnational citizenship is characterized by "growth of diasporic communities; and cultural hybridity as an aspect of mainstream political life" (Turner 2006, 23). Diasporic communities are communities of individuals from the same ethnic, cultural, or religious group who congregate in new parts of the world but retain their ties to one another and to their place of origin. Cultural hybridity refers to their adoption of new cultural norms at the same time as they retain their older norms and customs, sometimes in modified form. For example, some non-Christians who emigrate to North America set up Christmas trees and give Christmas presents to please their American- or Canadian-born children.

However, these hybrid, diasporic communities are often biased toward the better off, those who can afford to migrate legally to new countries. In the new transnational class system, unskilled laborers and the unemployed poor have far less chance to migrate legally. Most

governments of prosperous nations still strictly control their immigra-
tion and refugee policies, in part because many citizen workers object
to competition from immigrants. For the poor, then, globalization often
means the insecurity of illegal migration and vulnerability to human
traffickers (Brysk and Shafir 2004). Indeed, Bauman refers to the victims of globalization as "human waste," noting that those who cannot
find jobs in the new economy are without any place in the new world, as
they cannot migrate to new "dumping grounds" for surplus humanity
the way "surplus" Europeans migrated during the Industrial Revolution
(2006, 40). This deliberately harsh language reflects the harsh reality of
life for those rendered surplus to globalization. While professional and
managerial migrants may easily acquire extra citizenship rights, illegal
migrants and refugees may suffer from a citizenship gap, with no country to protect them (Brysk and Shafir 2004).

Confinement of the poor to their own borders seems a form of global
apartheid (Richmond 1994); those who are stateless or illegal migrants
have little recourse when their human rights are violated. Nor can the
poor claim to be refugees: the 1951 United Nations Convention Relating to the Status of Refugees mandates the right of individuals to claim
refugee status from political persecution, but it does not permit them
to claim refugee status because they suffer severe economic distress
(Brownlie and Goodwin-Gill 2006, 288–303). International human
rights law therefore seems stacked against those most likely to suffer
from globalization's detrimental effects.

The unbalanced nature of the class forces of international capitalism
suggests a highly differentiated capacity to adapt to the changing world.
To those in the business, governmental, or professional elite, liberal
political economies and individual human rights may seem very attractive, supporting their social and cultural adaptation to a global social
milieu. To those impoverished by globalization, adaptation to the new
environment is much more difficult. A culture of consumerism and a
social world of urban, individualistic competition may merely heighten
their sense of insecurity. It may also increase their resentment not only
against the West but also against the more privileged in their own societies, especially where globalization results in wider inequalities between

rich and poor. Such a downward spiral of human rights may verify the pessimistic model of globalization (figure 5.1).

CULTURAL CHANGE AND RESENTMENT OF THE WEST

Marshall McLuhan regarded earlier aspects of the compression of time and space now characteristic of globalization to be evidence of the formation of a global village (1962, 31). The notion of a global village is inaccurate, however. Village society is characterized by closeness and familiarity among residents—a thick feeling of community. The emerging international society of the twenty-first century is not a global village but a global city, with very thin if not nonexistent community feeling.

For some individuals, the city is a liberating place where social constraints are loosened and the obligations one bears are chosen, not ordained by family, kin, or communal group. These individuals often form communities of choice, based on social roles as much as if not more than family ties. The term "social role" applies to the diverse obligations and activities an individual might have, such as parent, worker, or participant in faith services; such social roles also reflect personal interests, such as one's volunteer or leisure activities. In cities, individuals in their diverse social roles often interact with people other than family members, sometimes developing sets of obligations to friends, coworkers, or others that can be as strong as their familial obligations. Often, their family, coworkers, and friends do not know one another, so the individual's social life takes place, and his set of communities emerges, within separate social networks.

But other individuals who live in cities do not develop new communities of choice, existing as mere strangers living together in a common space. With very high rates of geographical mobility, community ties are often lacking; one can choose to make the acquaintance of one's neighbor or coworker and assume obligations to him, or equally choose to ignore him. The narrow, filmy layer of commonality symbolized by shared taste in clothes, consumer goods, and mass media is not enough to create new communities of obligation.

Yet without communities of obligation, social life is a façade. Sociality implies not only choice but also willingness to take responsibility for others' well-being. Society implies a sense of collective morality (Saunders 1993, 68); when the cultural and communal bases of this morality erode, there is little of society left. Insofar as globalization promotes urbanization and international migration without the possibility of migrants creating or integrating into diasporic communities or new communities of choice, it promotes feelings of disconnection. These feelings are deeply exacerbated for migrants who cannot find work or who do not possess enough resources to create new families in their new places of residence.

The new technology that compresses space and time can generate social withdrawal as much as social connection, not only in cities but also internationally. Space is not genuinely compressed, nor does the capacity for instant and generalized communication necessarily result in greater assumption of social responsibility. Rorty (1993) suggests that sympathies are evoked by face-to-face communication, by tales of suffering that one can read on a face as one hears them recounted. If this is so, then some individuals may assume greater responsibilities to strangers when technology brings them closer together psychologically. Others, however, may simply regard greater access to knowledge about people in remote parts of the globe as a form of entertainment, to be switched on and off at will. The capacity for empathy engendered by actual personal contact among individuals is not generated to the same depth or sensitivity by technological contacts. Cynicism can replace sociality; people are more easily manipulated and used when face-to-face interaction is unnecessary. Globalization, then, may imply a new stage in the decline of the public. Individuals confine themselves to the private sphere, conducting their public life at a greater distance from one another than ever, if they indeed engage in public life at all (Sennett 1978). The global village begins to look like a global megalopolis with very few citizens making decisions, the rest deprived of or uninterested in influence.

Whether a force for intensified alienation or a force for new global activism, changes in the social world affect those already at risk from globalization. When loss of social norms, family, and community is added to loss of economic security, the individual may be cast adrift in a sea of uncertainty. Unable economically and educationally to enjoy urban life except perhaps via sex, drink, and drugs, many individuals experience severe loss of personal bearings. Their own cultures having been rooted in certainty, socially agreed-upon group norms, and prescribed family roles, they are now victims of the alienation that results from loss of their social role and loss of opportunity to engage in productive labor.

Without access to land, for example, tens of millions of young African men find it difficult to marry, as they cannot support a wife and children. They often turn to substitutes for their eroded cultures, whether to cults, magic, or political demagoguery. Increased poverty induced "frustration, anger, ignorance, despair and cynicism" among young men in pre-1994 Rwanda, making membership in the armed militias being trained to commit genocide an attractive option for many (Adelman 2000, 435). Rwanda's poverty was in part a consequence of globalization; the structural adjustment program that Rwanda had adopted resulted in declining social services and higher unemployment shortly before the genocide began (Uvin 1998, 58–59).

Individuals whose lives are disrupted by globalization are also susceptible to cultural retreat. Assertions of cultural particularity or even superiority arise as national cultures weaken and new cultural forms emerge that rely partly on myths of Western imperialism and resentment of social changes seemingly caused by contact with the West. Much is made of the new global culture of consumer goods. No matter where one travels, for example, one can find young people who understand the importance of being seen in the "right" clothes; even young men in Burma wear their baseball caps backward (Ash 2000, 21). To wear the right clothes signals an affinity with global culture, suggesting that one could merge easily into Western society if one only had the luck to get to the West. This is a thin culture, however; it relies on symbols to indicate affinities or preferences, but does not indicate a deep attachment to the values and social norms of liberal democracies. Certainly, material symbols of Westernization do not necessarily indicate acceptance of human rights.

Nations or elites trying to preserve their local cultures or what they believe their cultures ought to be resent the incursions of Western materialism. Western clothes, media, and music seem to presage the incursion of all Western values and customs, including human rights. Iranian president Mahmoud Ahmadinejad's claim 'at Columbia University in 2007 that "in Iran, we don't have homosexuals like in your country [the United States]" reflects this fear of Western influence (Ahmadinejad 2007); to him and others who oppose Western culture, homosexuality represents the antithesis of stable family relations (Howard-Hassmann 2001). This reaction is typical of many in the non-Western world who do not wish their societies to adopt the materialistic, crime- and gun-ridden values that seem to typify American life. As the elder statesman of Singapore, Lee Kuan Yew, said, "I find parts of it [America] totally unacceptable: guns, drugs, violent crime, vagrancy, unbecoming behavior in public—in sum the breakdown of civil society. The expansion of the right of the individual to behave or misbehave as he pleases has come at the expense of orderly society" (Zakaria 1994, 111).

This discussion does not acknowledge the reality of American, Iranian, or Singaporean ways of life. Homosexuality, which Ahmadinejad claimed was a Western phenomenon, is practiced in most societies in one form or another (Herdt 1997; Murray and Roscoe 1997). To the West's critics, however, it seems that Westerners believe that it is appropriate to bring into the public eye what any decent non-Westerner knows belongs in the private sphere. Westerners, it seems, have no shame, and Americans especially seem incapable of keeping even the most intimate, private aspects of human behavior out of the public realm. But others are equally culpable, such as the two British tourists accused of public indecency, being intoxicated in public, and having illicit sexual relations in public, after they were arrested on a beach in Dubai in July 2008 (McQueen 2008).

Global tourism upsets some of those non-Westerners attempting to preserve their own cultures; the entire world now seems vulnerable to the tourist gaze. Rich Western tourists stare at those less rich as objects— exoticized beings who exist to satisfy the tourists' curiosity and sense of excitement. The global tourist culture is also one of sexual predation, as Westerners fly to Thailand or Kenya to have sexual relations with young girls or boys. Here, again, it does not matter that Thai police and government officials actively connive at sex tourism (Bales 1999, 34–79). What matters is that wealthy foreigners invade local private spaces.

With the onslaught of Western material goods and mass media, moreover, it seems that local media risk being completely engulfed. Depictions of violence and sex seem to be the overwhelming favorites of ordinary citizens. Nor is this importation of Western "decadence" balanced by export of indigenous non-Western cultures to the Western world. While an international culture of music, dance, film, and literature has emerged as an attractive feature of globalization, much indigenous culture is filtered or mediated for Western consumption. To those who value creativity, such cultural mixing and cultural producers' eclectic use of whatever they encounter might signal a genuine world cultural community. Globalization frees people from the "tyranny of geography" so that they can enjoy art, music, literature, cuisine, and clothing from all parts of the world in whatever mixture they choose (Legrain 2002, 318). But to those who value purity, eclecticism spells danger; mixture is degradation, the conversion and mixing of local cultures into hybrid international consumer goods.

Freed from the direct cultural imperialism of the past, non-Western societies now face cultural diffusion—the voluntary adoption of Western cultural artifacts and practices. Hundreds of millions, if not billions, of citizens individually choose to adopt or emulate Western consumer goods, symbols, and ways of life, upsetting the "culturally fearful" (Sen 1999, 243). Human rights appear to be part of this general cultural emanation from the West, yet like the desire for other aspects of Western culture, governments cannot control the desire for human rights. Only a complete closing off of all borders, technical as well as physical, can slow down the process of cultural Westernization, including the demand for more individual human rights.

Among some individuals, this cultural change breeds nationalist resentment and attempts to return to local social purity and isolation. On the other hand, non-Westerners in general and Muslims in particular are divided in their views; the value of democracy, especially, is widely although not universally embraced in the non-Western world (Kohut and Wike 2008). Members of Islamist social movements in countries such as Algeria and Egypt may deeply resent the West but are not representative of local public opinion. Sudden, severe social change often is accompanied by local reaction, whether political, religious, or cultural, but such reaction does not always reflect popular social feelings.

THE POLITICS OF RESENTMENT AND INTEGRALIST REACTIONS

In the eyes of some non-Western elites, the promotion of universal human rights adds even more political and social strain to local cultures undergoing globalization. Nondemocratic, non-Western states are criticized for maintaining forms of political rule that might seem quite sensible to them or at least to certain of their elite members, and told that they should make themselves more Western. With extreme social disorder already evident, they are advised to permit even more disorder, it seems, in the form of freedom of speech, legal public protest, and legal social movements. With social solidarity declining, they are advised to give rights to women, children, and even homosexuals, eroding family and clan structure. They are also criticized if they do not allow free access to world—usually Western—media. Small wonder, then, that many segments of non-Western societies strongly resent what is seen as the Western call for human rights.

Samuel Huntington argued controversially in the 1990s that the risks of international advocacy of human rights outweighed the advantages. Huntington (1996) believed that the next great world conflict would result from clashes between civilizations with radically different values, including the values of human rights. McGrew agreed that "despite the hyperbole . . . Huntington is probably correct in asserting that human rights is today the critical faultline in an emerging cultural contestation of western globalization and hegemony" (1998, 200). Indeed, one of the aspects of Westernization that Osama bin Laden particularly resented was human rights. After the 9/11 attack on the World Trade Center, he said, "The values of this Western civilization under the leadership of America have been destroyed. These awesome symbolic towers that speak of liberty, human rights, and humanity have been destroyed. They have gone up in smoke" (Buruma and Margalit 2004, 13).

International polling data suggests, however, that the vast majority of Muslims disagree with bin Laden's view of human rights. The

majority support democracy (Inglehart and Norris 2003) and view economic aspects of globalization such as trade, foreign companies, and free
markets as positive, although many also believe that American policies are
responsible for the increasing disparity between rich and poor countries
(Kohut and Wike 2008). Moreover, while many Muslims polled in Jordan,
Lebanon, Indonesia, Turkey, Pakistan, and Kuwait in 2003 expressed confidence in bin Laden—and some continued to express confidence in him
as late as 2007—the majority rejected him as a possible political leader.
On the other hand, Muslims are uneasy about other human rights values,
especially equality of women, women's rights to abortion and divorce, and
tolerance of homosexuals (Kohut and Wike 2008). Indeed, it might be fair
to say that "the cultural fault line that divides the West and the Muslim
world is not about democracy but sex" (Inglehart and Norris 2003, 63).

Some critics speak of a perceived monolithic "Muslim" reaction
against the West as "Islamofascism," implying that those who seek to
maintain the Muslim community against the onslaught of Western values are fascist. This is an inflammatory word, connected in the Western intellectual lexicon with Nazism. A better term to describe such
anti-Western reaction as does exist is integralism, indicating a desire
to integrate individuals and society into one cohesive whole, without
the fractures, disjointedness, risk, and upset of social hierarchies that
accompany urban, industrial, and global life. In the integralist view, the
individual—especially the female individual—has one clear set of social
roles and a set place in the social hierarchy; society, politics, and the
economy are also all integrated into one orderly normative whole. Thus,
integralists resist the economic and social fragmentation characteristic
of the global age (Albrow 1997, 64). Integralism has characterized the
worldviews of intellectuals in many societies faced with large-scale social
change, from Russian agrarian romantics in the late nineteenth century
to Japanese and German nationalists in the twentieth, to Hindu nationalists in colonial India, to some Muslims and Christians today (Buruma
and Margalit 2004). In the Islamic world, integralists turn to the Qur'an
and shari'a law to explain each individual's place in society and how the
public realm should be ordered; in the West, Christian integralists turn
to the Bible and their religious leaders for the same reason.

It seems to integralist critics that the West has devised a social and political system that in principle protects individual human rights but does not always protect the community. Moreover, the West's unwillingness to acknowledge the damage it has caused to other societies weighs heavily on many people from non-Western countries. To such critics, it is easy for the West to preach human rights, which can be much more easily protected when a country is wealthy than when it is poor. Yet much Western wealth, critics believe, was accumulated by exploitation of the non-Western world. At issue here is not how the West actually developed but the perception that capitalism has always been the result of "conquest, enslavement, robbery, murder, briefly force," as Marx eloquently put it ([1867] 1967, 714). Strong social memories of colonial times (Sen 2006, 85) contribute to a general sense of humiliation at the hands of the free, prosperous West. With the right political impetus, these social memories can support violent reaction among those who now seem permanently dispossessed.

Non-Western countries do not encounter the disruptive social changes of the second great transformation from the same starting position as Western countries during the first. For many, the economic distortions of colonization and, in the case of Africa, the slave trade render it difficult to compete in the global marketplace. Without some form of acknowledgment of collective Western responsibility, not only for the crisis-ridden postcolonial period but also for emerging social problems in areas disrupted by global capitalism, human rights advocates may seem to be increasingly archaic remnants of Western imperialism. Culturalist resentment of the West might be ameliorated if Western states were more willing to acknowledge responsibility for past human rights violations they perpetrated in the rest of the world, and perhaps even issue some selective apologies; for example, in 2006 Tony Blair expressed sorrow for Britain's participation in the slave trade (Howard-Hassmann 2008, 141).

This suggestion does not mean that the West should abandon its human rights standards, nor does it mean that Western activists and analysts should abandon historical objectivity or absolve local states and elites of their own considerable responsibilities for human rights abuses in their own countries. Rather, the West should acknowledge its responsibility in creating the non-Western world that exists today. Sen believes that even if they do not approve of terrorism, many people tolerate it, "particularly where there is a sense of having been badly treated, for example, because of being left behind by global economic and social progress" (2006, 145). If this is so, then it is imperative as a matter of global human security not only to remedy current poverty and inequality, but also to address the sense of grievance against the West for its past exploitation of the non-Western world.

Nevertheless, adopting these measures will not be enough to contain the threat posed by the politics of resentment. Very few integralists are fascists; the vast majority do not espouse violence either against social deviants within their own societies or against outsiders. They do not want to leap backward, though some may wish to leap sideways (Zaidi 2009) into a more familiar world where there are still social protections against the economic insecurities and social distortions that globalization brings. A few integralists, however, are terrorists and pose a severe risk to human security. For the sake of their religious or cultural beliefs, they are willing to leap backward into history, forgoing human rights for their distorted interpretations of how both their local societies and the world political economy ought to be organized.

9

THE PRIMACY OF POLITICS

Critics of globalization look to different types of solutions to its adverse aspects. One proposed solution for inequality and poverty, whether they are caused by globalization or not, is redistribution of some of the world's resources. Another proposed solution is to institute domestic authoritarian socialism to control a country's relations with the world economy. The first solution is morally admirable but not entirely practical; the second is dangerous to both civil/political and economic human rights. Social democracy is the best political system for the protection of all human rights. However, serious threats to human security will remain, even in the unlikely event that most states begin to temper capitalism with social democracy.

WORLD REDISTRIBUTION VS. INTERNAL INSTITUTIONAL CHANGE

Even in the globalization era, the state bears the principal responsibility to ensure individuals' enjoyment of economic rights. However, many poorer states do not possess the resources necessary to ensure such enjoyment, even when the government is democratic and state elites are not self-interested. The national pie is very small. The international pie is much bigger, leading many human rights activists to suggest redistribution of the world's resources. Those who believe that the West accrued its wealth by actively underdeveloping its former colonies (Rodney 1972; Frank 1967) also believe there is a powerful moral case for redistribution.

One argument against world redistribution is that individuals do not bear obligations to remedy problems that they did not themselves cause. Narveson maintains that the current residents of the Western world did not cause world poverty; therefore, the world's poor may not call upon the wealthy West to assist them as a matter of right, although Westerners may choose to assist them as a matter of charity (1999, 143–56). Further, some argue that we bear more responsibility to the people closest to us than to distant others. There is "no general community of mankind" and "no person can respond to the full range of human misery," as Hoffmann summarizes this position (1981, 152). Thus, "compatriot favoritism" is a sensible way to order our obligations, our fellow citizens taking precedence over people who live in distant lands (Jones 1999, 111). The opposing viewpoint contends that we bear universal obligations; those whom we do not know and whose situation we have not at all influenced are as deserving of our concern as our own families (Singer 2004, 11–32).

Whatever philosophers may say, many individuals in the wealthy Western world are concerned about the poverty endured by distant others. They believe they have an obligation to assist the poor and that this obligation goes beyond the individual choice to contribute to charities. Yet a human being's capacity to feel a sense of community with strangers seems to be limited. Individuals have difficulty feeling that strangers have as much place in their "universe of obligation" (Fein 1979, 33) as do family, friends, and compatriots. For example, Canadian civic leaders whom I interviewed in 1996–97 explained that they found the obligations of humanitarian citizenship more indirect and harder to honor the farther away its objects were (Howard-Hassmann 2003, 200–214). Even the most engaged Western citizens are unlikely to donate more than what they consider their "fair share" to assist people in underdeveloped countries, and this fair share will not normally undermine their own standard of living.

Some suggestions for redistribution of world resources do not appear, at first glance, to ask Westerners to do more than their fair share. Pogge suggests that 1 percent of world income should be redistributed to the poor; in 2002 this figure amounted to $312 billion (2002, 205). If such redistribution did take place, however, it would entail enormous administrative and procedural difficulties analogous to the familiar problems connected to foreign aid. Several decades of Western foreign aid, amounting to $2.3 trillion since 1960 (Easterly 2006, 4), have done little to ameliorate poverty in the less developed world. Yet there may be ways to tax global economic transactions to generate funds for redistribution. Pogge suggests a Global Resources Dividend, a tax on the use of the world's resources no matter what country officially owns them (2002, 205–14). Others suggest taxes on financial flows, plane tickets, weapons exports, or CO_2 emissions (Milanovic 2005, 160).

Despite such suggestions for world redistribution, in practical terms alleviation of poverty requires the creation of societies that allow people to use their own resources and capacities to support themselves. Changes in economic, political, legal, and institutional arrangements within states can induce economic growth in poor countries and help them use their increased resources to guarantee their citizens' economic rights. At minimum, institutional arrangements must include democratic government, the rule of law, effective protection of private property, a regulated market economy, and basic provisions for social welfare. They must also include civil and political rights; economic justice means allowing individuals both the political and economic freedoms that enable them to stand on their own two feet. Globalization contributes both to institutional reform and to personal freedoms. With regard to economic institutional reform, it promotes free market economies that permit citizens to engage in domestic and international production, trade, and consumption. It contributes to political reform by spreading the ideals of civil and political rights, in part through the international human rights regime and in part through conditions for financial assistance required by IFIs. It also contributes to institutional reform by facilitating the spread of information and technology.

The necessity of internal institutional reform does not imply that the West should completely eschew concrete financial measures that could assist poor countries. Some countries do need foreign aid and debt relief, and wealthy countries should give it, if only in their own self-interest to prevent the political reactions against the wealthy discussed in chapter 8. The international human rights regime must also be strengthened to oblige both TNCs and IFIs to fulfill their human rights obligations. The globalized world is one in which states have less effective economic sovereignty than in earlier eras; the global legal and regulatory regime must therefore substitute for states' lack of instruments to fully protect their citizens' economic human rights. The responsibility to provide a social safety net for those whose economic human rights are undermined by globalization is a global, not only a local, matter.

In the real world of politics, however, the type of regime under which an individual lives is still the most important determinant of whether she enjoys her human rights. World social democracy is the best political regime to control the nefarious effects of globalization. Yet in the meantime, some states might turn to alternative political systems.

A RETURN TO SOCIALISM?

In some countries, a quasi-socialist escape from the world market may be an attractive option. Despite the known inefficiencies of nonmarket economies, the dream of a noncompetitive, cooperative world still appeals to many of globalization's critics. Socialism may seem the best guarantor of sovereignty, sociality, and subsistence, even if it demands the sacrifice of economic growth and even if Soviet-style socialism has been discredited.

In the late twentieth century, as societies hitherto outside the capitalist fold integrated into the world market, socialism as an economic system seemed completely discredited. By the early twenty-first century, only a few marginal states such as Burma, North Korea, and Cuba still clung to socialism, in all cases to the extreme economic detriment of their citizens. Both the Burmese and North Koreans starved. Formerly a rice-exporting country, Burma continued to produce a rice surplus in 2007, but its citizens were plagued by official corruption, lack of transport, and legal restrictions on travel, which prevented them from buying the rice they needed (*Economist* 2007c, 44). After the cyclone of May 2–3, 2008, hit Burma, its rulers rejected and stalled foreign assistance. North Koreans starved in the 1990s and continued to suffer from malnourishment in the twenty-first century, partly due to government economic policies that stifled private production of and private markets in food (Becker 2005; Haggard and Noland 2007).

Some critics of globalization regard Cuba as a successful socialist state. Cuba is a small country enjoying a favorable climate, whose ruler from 1959 until his resignation in 2008, Fidel Castro, seemed far less corrupt that many other dictators. Cuba has retained sovereignty over its economy despite a U.S. blockade since 1963. However, Cuba relied for three decades on Soviet aid; once the Soviet regime ended, Russia was no longer interested in assisting it. Although Cubans enjoy a good physical quality of life according to such measures as literacy rates and infant and child mortality rates, they are heavily dependent on scanty government rations. Sociality in Cuba is enforced by poverty. The limitations on the internal market economy and on international market relations imposed by both their own government and the U.S. blockade oblige Cubans to rely heavily on tourism—including sex tourism—for foreign exchange. Without the right to protest government policies, moreover, ordinary Cubans cannot make their concerns known except through indirect means.

Despite these examples of socialism's economic failures, the perceived detrimental effects of global capitalism on national economies are so severe that socialism, or at least a populist version of it, appeared to be making a comeback in Latin America in the early twenty-first century. Populism is characterized by political leaders' appeals to the underprivileged "masses" of their citizens; these appeals frequently rely on a personal relationship between a charismatic leader and his followers, rather than on any sort of policy platform (Sandbrook et al. 2007, 28). They are also often based on fears of an identifiable "other" who allegedly possesses inordinate economic power. The other against whom populist leaders urge their citizens to strive in the twenty-first century is usually the American. The insecurities generated by the international market, social change, new technologies, and the imperative to migrate in search of a living are all attributed to a capitalist plot led by the United States.

Latin Americans have good reason to believe in a capitalist American plot, given the American government's policies in the region from the 1950s to the 1990s. The United States boycotted Cuba, which at least provided basic education and medical care to its citizens, even if other aspects of its socialist economic planning caused more harm than good. The United States also fought a war against the Sandinistas in Nicaragua, who were trying to emulate the Cuban example in the 1980s. At the same time, the United States supported other governments that engaged in state terror and even genocide, as in the case of Chile, Argentina, and Guatemala. Nevertheless, globalization is too complex—indeed, too global—a phenomenon to ascribe all of its consequences to American policies.

In the early twenty-first century, President Hugo Chávez of Venezuela attempted to control his country's relations with the world capitalist economy; he believed that he could use Venezuela's vast oil reserves to improve the national standard of living. However, he sold much oil at heavily subsidized prices to his own citizens when he could have sold it at higher prices on the international market and used the profits to invest in the country's future. He also imposed price controls on staple goods, resulting in food shortages as producers lacked incentives to sell at low prices (*Economist* 2007d, 31). Although Venezuelans did see improvements in their living standards, it was unclear whether they resulted from Chávez's policies or merely from the wealth generated by the temporary increase in world oil prices; by 2009 falling oil prices were substantially undermining Chávez's capacity to use the national wealth to raise living standards. Chávez also attempted to consolidate his power in ways that suggested he might become a dictator. On December 2, 2007, a proposal that would have given him the right to be elected president in perpetuity was barely defeated in a referendum. Extremely averse to any criticism, in September 2008 Chávez expelled two researchers from Human Rights Watch who had traveled to Caracas, the capital city, to present a report on human rights in Venezuela (Vivanco and Wilkinson 2008).

Additionally, Chávez used Venezuelan oil to help like-minded Latin American states. He instituted a system of barter trade with Cuba, which sent doctors to Venezuela in return for oil. This caused consternation among some Cubans who experienced reduced access to doctors, but joy among some poor Venezuelans who, for the first time, enjoyed medical treatment. Oil from Venezuela also helped support Nicaragua, one of the poorest countries in the Americas and one in which the business and investment communities were still treated with suspicion (Kinzer 2008). However, despite these attempts at regional cooperation, twenty-first-century populist socialism in Latin America seemed likely to encounter the same problems as its predecessors elsewhere in the world. Even the most benign socialist regime can make errors that cannot be rectified without democracy; when that democracy is further compromised by authoritarian tendencies, ordinary citizens suffer even more. Social democracy is therefore a far better type of political regime than populist socialism.

SOCIAL DEMOCRACIES

Social democracy is a variant of liberalism that views the social provision of economic security as an inherent part of respect for the individual (Howard 1995, 199). It is characterized by an activist state that that tries to provide basic social rights, protect citizens against market forces, and reduce inequality (Sandbrook et al. 2007, 69). Both civil and political freedoms associated with democracy and the economic protections associated with socialism are objectives of state policy; thus, the state regulates the market not only in the interests of efficient production and trade but also in the interests of its citizens' material needs. The state accepts its responsibility to ensure that everyone enjoys a minimum standard of living suitable to that particular society. The social ethos includes a high degree of collective responsibility for the general welfare, and there is a national commitment to public goods such as accessible and affordable educational institutions and health care. Citizens' economic security is a matter of entitlement, or right, not something that must be earned.

In effect, social democracies are welfare states. Welfare states are expensive, however; they require relatively high tax burdens on ordinary citizens and private corporations, and efficient and nondiscriminatory distributive policies by governments to support those who cannot support themselves. In the late twentieth century, many countries in Europe and North America cut welfare spending to avoid jeopardizing the future well-being of their national economies. Sometimes those who cut budgets tried to introduce the idea that receipt of welfare ought to be contingent on proof that the potential recipient was trying to find work, rather than being a citizen's entitlement. There were moves in both the United States and Canada in the 1990s to demand that persons receiving welfare payments show they were actively seeking work (Neubeck 2006; Howard-Hassmann 2003, 138–99). These problems suggest that fulfillment of economic rights by the state will always be difficult. Insofar as globalization contributes to economic growth, thereby providing states with more resources for distribution of economic benefits, it may potentially promote universal economic rights. States are unlikely to protect the economic rights of their citizens, however, unless the citizens also enjoy civil and political rights and a democratic political structure, which force their governments to pay attention to their economic rights.

In 1941 Franklin Delano Roosevelt, then president of the United States, called for four essential freedoms: freedom from want, freedom from fear, freedom of speech and expression, and freedom of worship (Howard-Hassmann and Welch 2006, 211). This call for four freedoms became a touchstone of the modern world, later incorporated into the Universal Declaration of Human Rights (UDHR). Roosevelt's call in his 1944 State of the Union Address for what could have become social democracy is less well known. In this address, he advocated many of the economic human rights later written into the 1948 UDHR and the 1966 International Covenant on Economic, Social, and Cultural Rights (ICESCR). Roosevelt advocated the right to a job; the right to earn enough money for food, clothing, and recreation; the right to a decent home; the right to adequate medical care; the right to a good education; and the right to protection from the "economic fears" of old age, sickness, accident, and unemployment. Roosevelt also called for the right of farmers to earn a decent living and the right of every businessman to "trade in an atmosphere of freedom from unfair competition and domination by monopolies at home or abroad" (Howard-Hassmann and Welch 2006, 213–14). These latter two freedoms should be of special interest to globalization's critics. If they were extended to the world stage, farmers and peasants would be able to earn a decent living and businessmen would be protected from unfair competition and monopolies, whether local or international.

Social democracies are market societies. To advocate social democracy is to reject the possibility that nonmarket economies can efficiently respect, protect, and fulfill economic human rights. As discussed in chapter 5, Sandbrook argues that markets are not "natural" and suggests that we ought to entertain the possibility of nonmarket societies based on reciprocity or redistribution (2000, 1074). Such societies would presumably reintroduce the sociability that, Polanyi contends, was destroyed in Europe by the first great transformation. Similarly, Nickel suggests that economies could be constructed based on rewards other than property, whether "income, prizes, or other personal property" (1987, 156). These rewards, however, do not encourage enterprising individuals to earn more money, save, and invest. They merely recreate a class society in which some can accumulate wealth or privilege without contributing to economic growth. Markets are natural; given the opportunity, most people will trade and most societies will develop some sort of currency to help them trade. Most people also want to accumulate property and have public authorities protect their property. The social democratic state accumulates the wealth needed for redistribution via taxation, not by confiscation of private property (the technique of communist states), nor by a populist "return" to economies based on barter or reciprocity.

Social democracies, then, are capitalist, and like liberal capitalist societies, they are based on protection of private property. Private property is not only a key aspect of neoliberal globalization policies; it simultaneously helps protect many individuals' economic human rights, allowing them to exercise their own economic capacities without fear of expropriation by governments. It assures them that their homes will not be bulldozed to the ground, their small enterprises destroyed, or their larger enterprises taken over for the benefit of corrupt government officials. Thus, the institution of private property was one of the key building blocks of Western capitalism. Despite its omission from the two key human rights covenants, private property ought to be considered a human right.

Not everyone can accumulate private property, nor can everyone support himself, even in a democratic market economy. Thus, social democracies must provide a basic floor of economic security for those unable to support themselves. Even Milton Friedman, renowned as the economist who rejected the 1930s New Deal redistribution in the United States in favor of a completely free market, accepted the state's obligation to care for the poor. He advocated a negative income tax to ensure that everyone had a guaranteed minimum income. Giving the poor the cash they needed would set a floor below which no one's income would fall without upsetting market relations (Friedman 1962, 191–92). Yet protection of the poor would not eradicate inequalities in wealth. Advanced market economies must tolerate some inequality; social leveling is unwise, as there must be material incentives for those who wish to innovate, or organize more efficient ways to produce goods.

Although the well-being of citizens in advanced capitalist democracies does not require complete income equality, it does require relative equality. Extreme social inequality violates the human dignity of the poor. Well-ordered, prosperous societies rely on a high degree of social trust, which in turn relies in part on relative equality. Individuals must not be so poor and degraded that they feel cast out of the community; rather, the poorest should be able to engage in public life along with the rich and have their voices heard. Thus, the widening inequality characteristic of the United States in the late twentieth and early twenty-first centuries (Friedman 2005, 350) undermines public discussion. When adults can find no jobs other than those that pay minimum wage, they often lack the time, resources, and self-respect necessary to participate in democratic debate.

Relative equality is not merely an ethical goal; it also contributes to economic growth. President Franklin Roosevelt realized that the American government had to provide jobs to overcome the economic depression of the 1930s. Eventually, federal programs supplied employment for eight million people (Friedman 2007, 26). Not only did these jobs feed and house families; they also provided them with income that could be spent, stimulating the production of more consumer goods. The argument of the 1930s still holds true: if people are so poor that they cannot buy, the economy as a whole is likely to suffer. Thus, during the economic crisis of 2008–9, citizens were urged to continue spending, and U.S. banks were lent funds by the government so that they could continue lending to consumers. Similarly, social safety nets contribute to economic growth because they ensure that all citizens enjoy a decent level of health and education, which is necessary if they are to contribute to the economy. These arguments also apply at the global level. It is in the collective interest for the world's poor to become wealthier, although it may not be in the individual interests of those who employ some of the poor.

Those who rhetorically oppose the spread of global capitalism often refer to the United States as an example the "rest" should not follow. The gap between rich and poor in the United States is considerably wider than in most developed Western countries. For example, in 2000 the ratio of income of the richest 10 percent of the U.S. population to the poorest 10 percent was 15:1, as compared to 8.3:1 in Canada (World Bank 2008a). Since 1948 income inequality in the United States moved "substantially upward under Republican presidents but slightly downward under Democrats" (Blinder 2008), suggesting that government policies do affect how the poor fare. While Republicans are more likely to favor tax reductions for the rich, Democrats are more likely to raise minimum wages and less likely to show hostility to trade unions (Blinder 2008). Other Western countries have more egalitarian income distribution than the United States, in part because of stronger histories of political organization by workers. Communist parties and Communist-controlled trade unions influenced social policy in countries such as France. Not all Western countries are based on the competitive, individualistic ethos that seems to pervade American culture. Many have a more communitarian attitude and accept that the wealthy are responsible for the well-being of the poor—hence their willingness to institute welfare states.

One significant question regarding globalization, then, is whether it can contribute to the development of social democratic states in the poorer parts of the globe. Sandbrook and his colleagues offer examples of three upper-middle-income countries, as classified by the World Bank (World Bank 2008b), and one state in India, a lower-middle-income country, that have been able to create social democracies: Costa Rica in Central America; Mauritius, an African island economy; Chile (since

1990); and the state of Kerala in India (Sandbrook et al. 2007). Costa Rica has the longest history of uninterrupted democracy. Chile's road to social democracy was in part paved by a decade and a half of capitalist reform accompanied by brutal repression of political dissidents. Mauritius was an early adopter of export-led growth that benefited from a strong state bequeathed by its former colonial rulers. Kerala has periodically enjoyed governments incorporating communist and socialist political parties, which invested heavily in health and education.

All four of these cases are capitalist societies integrated into the global market economy. All have relatively strong states, contradicting critics' concern that globalization necessarily undermines local state autonomy. The political elites who control these states use government policy to regulate their integration into the world market. All four cases possess strong social democratic political parties committed to growth with equity and welfarist redistribution, principles that the national elites also accept. Partly via social democratic parties, workers are integrated into the state and trade unions are important political actors. Peasants are politically and socially represented. Civil society also plays an active role in defense of human rights (Sandbrook et al. 2007). In effect, these four societies are empirical illustrations of the ideal-type diagrams of the development of rights-protective societies presented in chapters 4 and 7. They are societies whose political elites use their sovereignty to protect citizens' economic human rights and which encourage a modern form of sociality embedded in formal political, labor, and civil society organizations.

Above all, each of these cases involved a class compromise. States did not dispossess property-owning landlords or capitalist entrepreneurs; rather, they negotiated with them (Sandbrook et al. 2007). Keeping the rich on the side of the government is necessary, even as reforms are instituted. When Chile went too far in the direction of socialism from 1970 to 1973, the result was a capitalist revolt supported by the United States. But even if there had been no outside threat, keeping the rich content is necessary for both economic growth and democratic politics. As Barrington Moore Jr. (1966) famously argued, without a bourgeoisie there cannot be democracy.

Yet if the bourgeoisie, the agent of capitalism, is necessary for democracy, it is hardly sufficient for human rights. In a large-scale quantitative study, Arat found that civil and political rights "cannot be sustained absent a minimum level of socio-economic rights" (1991, 103); below that level, the democratic protection of civil and political rights loses political legitimacy. Capitalism alone, unmediated by redistributive policies, cannot ensure economic human rights for all; thus, social democracies must restrain the predatory aspects of capitalism and ensure that accumulated national wealth is spread among all social classes. Trust between social classes is another necessary component of social democratic societies, and it is more likely to exist when all enjoy the benefits of economic growth, even if unequally. If this trust does not exist, then it is easy for populist leaders to rouse the excluded classes against democratic capitalist regimes. Populist regimes that use reactionary, anticapitalist, or anti-Western rhetoric to encourage distrust of local or international bourgeoisies may well encourage global threats to human security rather than global social democracy.

THREATS TO HUMAN SECURITY

The term "human security" emerged in the 1990s as a response to new or more generalized global "downside risks" (Fukuda-Parr 2003, 167; United Nations Development Programme 1994). These new risks included terrorism, environmental damage, crime, trafficking in drugs and people, new diseases, and sudden economic downswings, including "instability and contagion in financial markets" (Fukuda-Parr 2003, 174). Everyone, rich and poor, in the north or south, was vulnerable to these risks.

The threat of sudden economic downswings to human security was made frighteningly clear in fall 2008, as this book was being completed. The entire world entered what seemed likely to become a severe international recession; many feared a repeat of the depression of the 1930s. The immediate precipitating cause of the recession appeared to be deregulation of the American financial and banking sectors, which had been occurring since the 1980s. This deregulation continued during the two administrations of President George W. Bush (2001–9), along with lack of regulation of trade in new kinds of financial securities in both the American and international markets. The decision to allow subprime mortgage lending was especially culpable in creating the financial crisis. Millions of homebuyers in the United States had taken on mortgages at interest rates below prime, against houses that were valued significantly above what the market later dictated their value to be. These homebuyers were at very high risk of default, as their mortgage debt often exceeded the value of the house they had bought. This ultimately unrepayable mortgage debt was then sold and resold in the international markets.

Moreover, deregulation of other sectors meant that banks were not required to hold enough cash assets to cover their loans in the event that those loans were recalled. Investment houses and insurance companies also bought this bad debt. Many countries followed the American example, deregulating the financial sector. Furthermore, ostensibly to encourage innovation, neither the Americans nor other countries regulated new financial products. Exacerbating these financial problems, during the Bush administration the U.S. government built up huge deficits, as opposed to the more careful fiscal and monetary policies of the Clinton administration.

The American government responded to this massive financial crisis in September 2008 by designating $750 billion in public funds to assist banks, investment houses, and insurance companies to weather the anticipated recession; in February 2009 the new Obama administration injected another $787 billion into the economy. In November 2008 the Bush administration also convened an international conference of the G20 states (the major industrial and industrializing states) to consider new international measures to regulate the financial sector, with many commentators noting that although the financial sector had rapidly globalized during the preceding two decades, regulatory measures remained national. The global financial sector included new financial instruments that were in no way controlled by national governments; for example, they were not taxed.

At the time of the writing of this book, the outcome of these new policies could not be predicted, but it seemed clear that the "free" market deregulation and nonregulation of the financial sector had to be immediately remedied. As a result of the financial crisis, the economies of many countries were expected to contract in 2009, and the World Bank predicted that the crisis would push 53 million more people in poor countries into extreme poverty (*Economist* 2009, 81). What remained to be seen was whether the financial crisis would permanently reduce the incomes of the hundreds of millions of people whose living standards had risen during the previous three decades of globalization. If such permanent impoverishment occurs, then critics of capitalism might have a much stronger case against globalization than this book has suggested. On the other hand, had globalization not taken place, the financial crisis might have pushed the world's less industrialized countries into an even worse position than they found themselves enduring after 2008.

Aside from sudden economic downswings like the one experienced in 2008–9, other threats to human security are a consequence of, or intersect with, globalization. The global spread of industrialization threatens the environment. Air travel facilitates the spread of new diseases. Trafficking in drugs and people reflects both ease of transport and travel and the desire of some individuals in the poorer parts of the world to move to the richer parts, even at the risk of enslavement.

The human security agenda stresses freedom from want and freedom from fear, not coincidentally reiterating Roosevelt's 1941 speech on the four freedoms (United Nations Development Programme 1994, 24). Freedom from want is a central part of the human rights agenda, as the ICESCR makes clear. If globalization results in fewer rather than more economic opportunities for ordinary citizens, then it directly assaults their freedom from want. If globalization causes increasing competition for economic goods between classes, genders, ethnic groups, countries, or regions, it also undermines freedom from fear. Fear is exacerbated during economic crises when governments introduce authoritarian policies and controls on the exercise of civil and political rights. The resultant social distrust undermines both citizens' ability to interact in a profitable manner in local and global markets and their ability to join together against exclusivist social movements and repressive political regimes.

But uncontrolled antiglobalization can also threaten human security. The politics of resentment infiltrates the relationship between much of the non-Western world and the West. The West is seen as the embodiment of globalization; globalization in turn is seen as imperialism in a new guise. The West, it seems, undermines local economies at the same time as it demands conformity to a political model of freedom and democracy that undermines such local traditions as the subordination of women to men. Some Western critics of globalization agree with this characterization of the West and, in an excess of moral relativism, attempt to defend all non-Western societies against globalization, whatever their internal cultural or political characteristics.

One political response to "Westernizing" globalization is terrorism. The anger generated by the decline of the social during the second great transformation seems to have contributed to public support for Al-Qaeda in some parts of the world. Resentment of the West is fuelled by a sense of hopelessness, especially among young, landless, and unemployed men who find themselves in a society of "capitalism without work" (Turner 2006, 73). The global erosion of male social roles can easily result in the glorification of one of the last male domains—that of violence. Some young men turn to a violent politics of resentment, such as membership in extremist Islamist movements, as a means of "symbolic empowerment" (Turner 2006, 85–86). It is not clear whether the actual terrorists emerge from this class of underemployed young men, even though it is commonly assumed that inequality and poverty are at terrorism's roots (Ehrlich and Liu 2002). Many terrorists are educated, and some, like Osama bin Laden himself, are from middle-class or even elite families. They appear to be driven more by an ideological anti-Westernism encouraged by some religious and political leaders than by any sense of personal hopelessness.

In any case, alienation is as much a result of lack of integration into global society as of integration. Two regions where many experience alienation are sub-Saharan Africa and the Middle East. Young men in sub-Saharan Africa are among the bottom billion; they live in states that do not play significant roles in the global economy, except sometimes as possessors of resources to be extracted by foreign-based TNCs in collaboration with local predator elites. The Middle East suffers from a deficit of political globalization—that is, of the civil and political rights that can assist citizens to both exercise their capacities to support themselves and resist political oppression. There is an indirect negative connection between globalization and transnational terrorism: when globalization promotes economic development, terrorism is less likely (Li and Schaub 2004; Robison, Crenshaw, and Jenkins 2006).

Thus, the antiglobalization movement can also constitute a risk to human security if in its zeal to counter the adverse effects of globalization—labeled Westernization or Americanization—it rejects political and economic liberalization. Insofar as, like its nineteenth-century predecessors, the antiglobalization movement points out the inequities and unfairness of capitalism and demands reform, it is an extremely valuable part of the globalization process. Insofar as it links up with the politics of resentment, it is dangerous. Like governments, IOs, and TNCs, social movements have political agendas. While many such agendas focus on human betterment, sometimes activists make mistakes in judgment that can have adverse consequences, just as the communist movement that arose during the first great transformation had adverse consequences. One such mistake in judgment is to blame globalization for the decisions of local actors and states. Another is to assume that capitalism and the global economy can have only harmful effects on human rights.

HUMAN RIGHTS LEAPFROGGING

In the game of leapfrog, little children crouch in a row, then leap over one another's backs, the child at the end starting first. In the human rights world, rights now leap over much larger obstacles. Oceans are crossed and centuries ignored as all regions engage in a giant debate about what human rights are or ought to be, what people from different parts of the world are entitled to, and who or what agencies are expected to respect or implement those rights. Over the Atlantic and Pacific Oceans, the

Mediterranean and Black Seas, human rights leap from rich to poor countries. Over the centuries of the first great transformation, human rights leap to the second great transformation. Those who are most deprived demand to leap to the head of the line. They demand all the rights to which they are entitled under international law, despite the relative economic, political, and legal underdevelopment of their own societies. And despite efforts by political and cultural spokespersons of various kinds to shut down borders, those suffering human rights abuses increasingly do hear the voices of human rights defenders.

While human rights leapfrogging promotes rights, it is itself an aspect of globalization to which many object. Reflecting the changes that occurred in Polanyi's Britain in the eighteenth and nineteenth centuries, human rights are posited upon the basic civil and political rights that authoritarian political systems frequently deny: namely, freedoms of speech, assembly, press, and association. Human rights are also posited upon a zone of personal privacy in family relations, economic activities, and individual decision making. To some people trying to protect their own societies, religions, and cultures from the homogenizing tendencies of globalization, the global norms that human rights activists propose seem suspiciously like "Western" norms. Some influential individuals in the developing world believe the human rights movement promotes a foreign normative system that requires social and cultural, as well as political, legal, and economic, change. The charge of cultural imperialism is frequently heard and the politics of resentment is manipulated to hold back the tide of human rights.

Thus, although human rights leapfrogging is one positive aspect of globalization, it is no guarantor of ultimate global respect for human rights. The fact that over the course of two centuries the capitalist West gradually became wealthy, relatively free, and democratic does not mean all other societies will inevitably do likewise. Nevertheless, globalization has spread the idea of human rights worldwide, intersecting with social changes on the ground.

Globalization, then, is a powerful tool for promotion of human rights. But whether in the end it will have promoted human rights more than it undermined them cannot be predicted. It is no more sensible to pass final judgment now on globalization as an instrument of social change than it would have been to pass judgment on the Industrial Revolution in 1780. Now, as then, the short-term detrimental consequences are obvious and humanitarians must strive to overcome the harms of dispossession, unemployment, and poverty. The longer-term benefits of globalization are harder to identify. Although we cannot predict globalization's final outcome, we must take seriously the economic and other data suggesting that it is having a positive effect in many regions of the world. The economic downturn of 2008–9 does not mean this progress is ephemeral.

While it might seem facile to argue that the trick is in the balance, only moderate approaches that both encourage economic growth and individual material betterment and simultaneously discourage economic exploitation and erosion of civil and political human rights can result, in the long run, in a world in which social democracy, with its commitment to the protection of all human rights, is the norm. The West, capitalism, and globalization should be criticized, but not vilified. Similarly, the non-Western world now undergoing globalization should be defended, but not romanticized. Human rights are an intensely political matter; all states and all governments, all international organizations and all private corporations, should be held accountable to the international standards of human rights.

REFERENCES

Aaronson, Susan Ariel. 2007. Seeping in slowly: How human rights concerns are penetrating the WTO. *World Trade Review* 6 (3): 1–37.

Abouharb, M. Rodwan, and David Cingranelli. 2007. *Human rights and structural adjustment.* New York: Cambridge University Press.

Acemoglu, Daron, and James A. Robinson. 2006. *Economic origins of dictatorship and democracy.* New York: Cambridge University Press.

Adelman, Howard. 2000. Rwanda revisited: In search for lessons. *Journal of Genocide Research* 2 (3): 431–44.

Ahmadinejad, Mahmoud. 2007. Iran's president at Columbia University: A transcript. *Arizona Daily Star,* September 25. http://www.azstarnet.com/sn/printDs/202820.

Ahrend, Rudiger. 2006. Russia's post-crisis growth: Its sources and prospects for continuation. *Europe-Asia Studies* 58 (1): 1–24.

Albrow, Martin. 1997. *The global age: State and society beyond modernity.* Stanford: Stanford University Press.

Arat, Zehra F. 1991. *Democracy and human rights in developing countries.* Boulder, Colo.: Lynne Rienner.

Arat, Zehra F. Kabasakal. 2006. Looking beyond the state but not ignoring it: A framework of analysis for non-state actors and human rights. In *Non-state actors in the human rights universe,* ed. G. Andreopoulos, Z. F. K. Arat, and P. Juviler. Bloomfield, Conn.: Kumarian Press.

Ash, Timothy Garton. 2000. Beauty and the beast in Burma. *New York Review of Books,* May 25, 21–25.

Associated Press. 2008. Troops fire on rioters in Somalia, killing 2. May 6. http://www.nytimes.com/2008/05/06/world/africa/06somalia.html.

Atleson, James B. 2006. International labor rights and North American labor law. In *Economic rights in Canada and the United States,* ed. R. E. Howard-Hassmann and C. E. Welch Jr. Philadelphia: University of Pennsylvania Press.

Baehr, Peter. 1994. Amnesty International and its self-imposed limited mandate. *Netherlands Quarterly of Human Rights* 12 (1): 5–21.

———. 2003. Human rights NGOs and globalization. In *Responding to the human rights deficit: Essays in honour of Bas de Gaay Fortman,* ed. K. Arts and P. Mihyo. The Hague, Netherlands: Kluwer Law International.

Bales, Kevin. 1999. *Disposable people: New slavery in the global economy.* Berkeley and Los Angeles: University of California Press.

Barber, Benjamin R. 1995. *Jihad vs. McWorld: How globalism and tribalism are reshaping the world.* New York: Ballantine Books.

Bauman, Zygmunt. 1998. *Globalization: The human consequences.* New York: Columbia University Press.

———. 2006. The crisis of the human waste disposal industry. In *The globalization of racism,* ed. D. Macedo and P. Gounari. Boulder, Colo.: Paradigm.

Becker, Jasper. 2005. *Rogue regime: Kim Jong Il and the looming threat of North Korea.* New York: Oxford University Press.

Beetham, David. 1998. Human rights as a model for cosmopolitan democracy. In *Re-imagining political community: Studies in cosmopolitan democracy,* ed. D. Archibugi, D. Held, and M. Kohler. Stanford: Stanford University Press.

Bello, Walden. 2008. Manufacturing a food crisis. *Nation,* June 2, 16–21.

Besley, Timothy, and Robin Burgess. 2003. Halving global poverty. *Journal of Economic Perspectives* 17 (3): 3–22.

Bhagwati, Jagdish. 2004. *In defense of globalization.* New York: Oxford University Press.

Bhalla, Surjit S. 2002. *Imagine there's no country: Poverty, inequality, and growth in the era of globalization.* Washington, D.C.: Institute for International Economics.

Blinder, Alan S. 2008. Is history siding with Obama's economic plan? *New York Times,* August 31. http://www.nytimes.com/2008/08/31/business/31view.html.

Bloem, Renate, Isolda Agazzi Ben Attia, and Philippe Dam. 2008. The Conference of NGOs (CONGO): The story of strengthening civil society engagement with the United Nations. In *Critical mass: The emergence of global civil society,* ed. J. W. St. G. Walker and A. S. Thompson. Waterloo, Canada: Wilfrid Laurier University Press.

Blowfield, Michael. 2007. Reasons to be cheerful? What we know about CSR's impact. *Third World Quarterly* 28 (4): 683–95.

Bob, Clifford. 2002. Globalization and the social construction of human rights campaigns. In *Globalization and human rights,* ed. A. Brysk. Berkeley and Los Angeles: University of California Press.

Bohman, James. 1999. International regimes and democratic governance: Political equality and influence in global institutions. *International Affairs* 75 (3): 499–513.

Bourguignon, François, and Christian Morrisson. 2002. Inequality among world citizens: 1820–1992. *American Economic Review* 92 (4): 727–44.

Bradsher, Keith, and Andrew Martin. 2008. World's poor pay price as crop research is cut. *New York Times,* May 18. http://www.nytimes.com/2008/05/18/business/worldbusiness/18focus.html.

Brown, Michael Barratt. 1974. *The economics of imperialism.* Harmondsworth, U.K.: Penguin.

Brownlie, Ian, and Guy S. Goodwin-Gill, eds. 2006. *Basic documents on human rights.* 5th ed. New York: Oxford University Press.

Brysk, Alison. 2005. *Human rights and private wrongs: Constructing global civil society.* New York: Routledge.

Brysk, Alison, and Gershon Shafir. 2004. *People out of place: Globalization, human rights, and the citizenship gap.* New York: Routledge.

Buruma, Ian, and Avishai Margalit. 2004. *Occidentalism: The West in the eyes of its enemies.* New York: Penguin Press.

Bush, George W. 2002. Remarks to the World Affairs Councils of America Conference. January 16. *Weekly Compilation of Presidential Documents* 38 (3): 78.

Business and Human Rights Resource Centre. 2008. Companies with human rights policies referring to the Universal Declaration of Human Rights. http://www.business-humanrights.org/Categories/Companypolicysteps/Policies/Companieswithhumanrightspolicies/Companyhumanrights policiesreferringtoUniversalDeclarationofHumanRights.

Buxton, Nick. 2004. Debt cancellation and civil society: A case study of Jubilee 2000. In *Fighting for human rights,* ed. P. Gready. New York: Routledge.

Cavanagh, John, and Jerry Mander, eds. 2004. *Alternatives to economic globalization: A better world is possible.* 2nd ed. San Francisco: Berrett-Koehler.

Central Intelligence Agency. 2008. World Factbook. https://www.cia.gov/library/publications/the-world-factbook/geos/wa.html.

Chen, Martha Alter. 1996. Engendering world conferences: The international women's movement and the UN. In *NGOs, the UN, and global governance,* ed. T. G. Weiss and L. Gordenker. Boulder, Colo.: Lynne Rienner.

Chen, Shaohua, and Martin Ravallion. 2001. How did the world's poorest fare in the 1990s? *Review of Income and Wealth* 47 (3): 283–300.

———. 2008. The developing world is poorer than we thought, but no less successful in the fight against poverty. Policy Research Working Paper 4703, World Bank Development Research Group. http://www-wds.world bank.org/external/default/WDSContentServer/IW3P/IB/2009/08/05/000158349_20090805133945/Rendered/PDF/WPS4703.pdf.

Chesterman, Simon. 2008. Globalization rules: Accountability, power, and the prospects for global administrative law. *Global Governance* 14 (1): 39–52.

Chua, Amy. 2004. *World on fire: How exporting free market democracy breeds ethnic hatred and global instability.* New York: Anchor Books.

Clapham, Andrew. 2006. *Human rights obligations of non-state actors.* New York: Oxford University Press.

Clark, Ann Marie. 2001. *Diplomacy of conscience: Amnesty International and changing human rights norms.* Princeton, N.J.: Princeton University Press.

Clark, Dana L. 2002. The World Bank and human rights: The need for greater accountability. *Harvard Human Rights Journal* 15:205–26.

Collier, Paul. 2007. *The bottom billion: Why the poorest countries are failing and what can be done about it.* New York: Oxford University Press.

Commission on Legal Empowerment of the Poor. 2008. *Making the law work for everyone.* Vol. 1. New York: CLEP and United Nations Development Programme.

Cooper, Andrew F. 2008. *Celebrity diplomacy.* Boulder, Colo.: Paradigm.

Danies, Joel. 2003. Explanation of vote: Right to development. U.S. Representative to the UN Human Rights Commission. Summary Record of the 63rd Meeting, 59th Sess., April 25. http://www.humanrights.usa.net/statements/0425RtoD.htm.

Dashwood, Hevina S. 2007. Canadian mining companies and corporate social responsibility: Weighing the impact of global norms. *Canadian Journal of Political Science* 40 (1): 129–56.

Davies, James B., Susanna Sandstrom, Anthony Shorrocks, and Edward N. Wolff. 2006. *The world distribution of household wealth.* Unpublished paper. December 5. www.iariw.org/papers/2006/davies.pdf.

Davies, Robert. 2003. The business community: Social responsibility and corporate values. In *Making globalization good: The moral challenges of global capitalism,* ed. J. H. Dunning. New York: Oxford University Press.

Deaton, Angus. 2004. Measuring poverty in a growing world (or measuring growth in a poor world). Unpublished paper, Research Program in Development Studies, Woodrow Wilson School of Public and International Affairs, Princeton University.

de Onis, Mercedes, Edward A. Frongillo, and Monika Blossner. 2000. Is malnutrition declining? An analysis of changes in levels of child malnutrition since 1980. *Bulletin of the World Health Organization* 78 (10): 1222–33.

de Senarclens, Pierre. 2003. The politics of human rights. In *The globalization of human rights,* ed. J.-M. Coicaud, M. W. Doyle, and A.-M. Gardner. Tokyo: United Nations University Press.

De Soto, Hernando. 2002. *The mystery of capital: Twenty-first Morgenthau Memorial Lecture on Ethics and Foreign Policy.* New York: Carnegie Council on Ethics and World Affairs.

Dicklitch, Susan. 1998. *The elusive promise of NGOs in Africa: Lessons from Uganda.* New York: St. Martin's Press.

Dicklitch, Susan, and Rhoda E. Howard-Hassmann. 2007. Public policy and economic rights in Ghana and Uganda. In *Economic rights: Conceptual, measurement, and policy issues,* ed. S. Hertel and L. Minkler. New York: Cambridge University Press.

Doctors Without Borders/Médecins Sans Frontières. 2009. About us: History and principles. http://www.doctorswithoutborders.org/aboutus/.

Dollar, David, and Aart Kraay. 2002. Spreading the wealth. *Foreign Affairs* 81 (4): 120–33.

Donnelly, Jack. 1989. *Universal human rights in theory and practice.* Ithaca, N.Y.: Cornell University Press.

———. 1999. Human rights, democracy, and development. *Human Rights Quarterly* 21 (3): 608–32.

———. 2003. *Universal human rights in theory and practice.* 2nd ed. Ithaca, N.Y.: Cornell University Press.

Drainville, André C. 2005. Quebec City 2001 and the making of transnational subjects. In *The global resistance reader,* ed. L. Amoore. New York: Routledge.

Du Plessis, Max. 2003. Historical injustice and international law: An exploratory discussion of reparation for slavery. *Human Rights Quarterly* 25 (3): 624–59.

Durkheim, Emile. 1933. *The division of labor in society.* New York: Free Press.

———. 1951. *Suicide: A study in sociology.* New York: Free Press.

Easterly, William. 2006. *The white man's burden: Why the West's efforts to aid the rest have done so much ill and so little good.* New York: Penguin Press.

Economist. 2007a. Cheap no more. December 8, 81–83.

———. 2007b. Emerging multinationals: They're behind you. December 8, 78.

———. 2007c. Myanmar: Misery piled upon misery. October 6, 44.

———. 2007d. The wind goes out of the revolution. December 8, 30–32.

———. 2008a. Cereal offenders. March 29, 98.

———. 2008b. Just good business: A special report on corporate social responsibility. January 19, 1–24.

———. 2008c. The new face of hunger. April 19, 31–34.

———. 2008d. The right time to chop. May 3, 15–18.

———. 2008e. The silent tsunami. April 19, 13.

———. 2009. Forgotten sibling. April 25, 81.

Ehrlich, Paul R., and Jianguo Liu. 2002. Some roots of terrorism. *Population and Environment* 24 (2): 183–91.

Eide, Asbjorn. 2006. Economic, social, and cultural rights as human rights. In *Human rights in the world community: Issues and actions,* ed. R. P. Claude and B. H. Weston. Philadelphia: University of Pennsylvania Press.

Englund, Harri. 2006. *Prisoners of freedom: Human rights and the African poor.* Berkeley and Los Angeles: University of California Press.

Evans, Tony. 2001. *The politics of human rights: A global perspective.* London: Pluto Press.

Falk, Richard. 1999. *Predatory globalization: A critique.* Cambridge, U.K.: Polity Press.

———. 2006. Global civil society actors and 9/11. In *Non-state actors in the human rights universe,* ed. G. Andreopoulos, Z. F. K. Arat, and P. Juviler. Bloomfield, Conn.: Kumarian Press.

Fein, Helen. 1979. *Accounting for genocide: National responses and Jewish victimization during the Holocaust.* Chicago: University of Chicago Press.

———. 2007. *Human rights and wrongs: Slavery, terror, genocide.* Boulder, Colo.: Paradigm.

Fitzpatrick, Joan. 2002. Book review. *American Journal of International Law* 96 (2): 501–4.

Fleshman, Michael. 2008. Africa struggles with soaring food prices. *Africa Renewal* 22 (2): 12–17.

Forsythe, David P. 1997. The United Nations, human rights, and development. *Human Rights Quarterly* 19 (2): 334–49.

———. 2006. *Human rights in international relations.* 2nd ed. Cambridge: Cambridge University Press.

Fortune. 2008. Fortune 500—global 500—top 10. http://money.cnn.com/magazines/fortune/global500/2008/full_list.

Fox, Jonathan. 2002. Transnational civil society campaigns and the World Bank Inspection Panel. In *Globalization and human rights,* ed. A. Brysk. Berkeley and Los Angeles: University of California Press.

Frank, Andre Gunder. 1967. *Capitalism and underdevelopment in Latin America: Historical studies of Chile and Brazil.* New York: Monthly Review Press.

Freeman, Michael. 2000. The perils of democratization: Nationalism, markets, and human rights. *Human Rights Review* 2 (1): 33–50.

———. 2002. *Human rights: An interdisciplinary approach.* Cambridge, U.K.: Polity Press.

Friedman, Benjamin M. 2002. Globalization: Stiglitz's case. *New York Review of Books,* August 15, 48–53.

———. 2005. *The moral consequences of economic growth.* New York: Vintage Books.

———. 2007. FDR and the Depression: The big debate. *New York Review of Books,* November 8, 26–29.

Friedman, Milton. 1962. *Capitalism and freedom.* Chicago: University of Chicago Press.

Fukuda-Parr, Sakiko. 2003. New threats to human security in the era of globalization. *Journal of Human Development* 4 (2): 167–79.

Fukuyama, Francis. 1989. The end of history? *National Interest,* Summer, 3–17.

———. 1999. The great disruption: Human nature and the reconstitution of social order. *Atlantic Monthly,* May, 55–80.

Gerth, H. H., and C. Wright Mills. 1958. The man and his work. Introduction to *From Max Weber: Essays in sociology,* by M. Weber, trans. H. H. Gerth and C. W. Mills. New York: Oxford University Press.

Gibb, Heather. 2003. Core labour standards: An incremental approach. In *Civilizing globalization: A survival guide,* ed. R. Sandbrook. Albany: State University of New York Press.

Gibney, Mark. 2005. *Five uneasy pieces: American ethics in a globalized world.* New York: Rowman and Littlefield.

———. 2008. *International human rights law: Returning to universal principles.* New York: Rowman and Littlefield.

Giddens, Anthony. 2003. *Runaway world: How globalization is reshaping our lives.* New York: Routledge.

Global Witness. 2006. The Kimberley Process at risk. *Global Witness,* November, 1–4. http://www.globalwitness.org/media.

Goldstein, Robert Justin. 1987. The United States. In *International handbook of human rights,* ed. J. Donnelly and R. E. Howard. New York: Greenwood Press.

Goodhart, Michael. 2005. *Democracy as human rights: Freedom and equality in the age of globalization.* New York: Routledge.

Goulet, Denis. 2005. Global governance, dam conflicts, and participation. *Human Rights Quarterly* 27 (3): 881–907.

Greenhill, Brian, Layna Mosley, and Aseem Prakash. 2008. Trade and labor rights: A panel study. Paper presented at the annual meeting of the American Political Science Association, Boston, August 28–31.

Greiden, William. 1981. The education of David Stockman. *Atlantic Monthly,* December. http://www.theatlantic.com/politics/budget/stockman.htm.

Grierson, Bruce, Kalle Lasn, and James MacKinnon. 1999–2000. WTO Seattle 99 (anti-globalization demonstrations). *Adbusters,* December–February, 64–66.

Griesgraber, Jo Marie. 2008. Influencing the IMF. In *Critical mass: The emergence of global civil society,* ed. J. W. St. G. Walker and A. S. Thompson. Waterloo, Canada: Wilfrid Laurier University Press.

Gunderson, James L. 2006. Multinational corporations as non-state actors in the human rights arena. In *Non-state actors in the human rights universe,* ed. G. Andreopoulos, Z. F. K. Arat, and P. Juviler. Bloomfield, Conn.: Kumarian Press.

Hafner-Burton, Emilie M. 2005. Right or robust? The sensitive nature of repression to globalization. *Journal of Peace Research* 42 (6): 679–98.

Haggard, Stephan, and Marcus Noland. 2007. *Famine in North Korea: Markets, aid, and reform.* New York: Columbia University Press.

Haskell, Thomas L. 1985. Capitalism and the origins of the humanitarian sensibility, part 2. *American Historical Review* 90:547–66.

He, Baogang, and Hannah Murphy. 2007. Global social justice at the WTO? The role of NGOs in constructing global social contracts. *International Affairs* 83 (4): 707–27.

Held, David, Anthony McGrew, David Goldblatt, and Jonathan Perraton. 1999. Globalization. *Global Governance* 5 (4): 483–96.

Held, David, et al. 2005. *Debating globalization.* Cambridge, U.K.: Polity Press.

Herdt, Gilbert. 1997. *Same sex, different cultures: Exploring gay and lesbian lives.* Boulder, Colo.: Westview Press.

Hertel, Shareen. 2005. What was all the shouting about? Strategic bargaining and protest at the WTO Third Ministerial Meeting. *Human Rights Review* 6 (3): 102–18.

———. 2006. *Unexpected power: Conflict and change among transnational activists.* Ithaca, N.Y.: Cornell University Press.

Hoffmann, Stanley. 1981. *Duties beyond borders: On the limits and possibilities of ethical international politics.* Syracuse: Syracuse University Press.

Hollander, Paul. 1995. *Anti-Americanism: Irrational and rational.* New Brunswick, N.J.: Transaction Press.

Horta, Korinna. 2002. Rhetoric and reality: Human rights and the World Bank. *Harvard Human Rights Journal* 15:227–43.

Howard, Rhoda E. 1986. *Human rights in Commonwealth Africa.* Totowa, N.J.: Rowman and Littlefield.

———. 1995. *Human rights and the search for community.* Boulder, Colo.: Westview Press.

Howard-Hassmann, Rhoda E. 2001. Gay rights and the right to a family: Conflicts between liberal and illiberal belief systems. *Human Rights Quarterly* 23 (1): 73–95.

———. 2003. *Compassionate Canadians: Civic leaders discuss human rights.* Toronto: University of Toronto Press.

———. 2008. *Reparations to Africa*. Philadelphia: University of Pennsylvania Press.

Howard-Hassmann, Rhoda E., and Claude E. Welch, eds. 2006. *Economic rights in Canada and the United States*. Philadelphia: University of Pennsylvania Press.

Human Rights Watch. 2008. *"One year of my blood": Exploitation of migrant construction workers in Beijing*. Human Rights Watch Report 20, no. 3(C). March. New York: Human Rights Watch. http://www.hrw.org/reports/2008/China0308/4.htm.

Huntington, Samuel P. 1996. *The clash of civilizations and the remaking of world order*. New York: Simon and Schuster.

Inglehart, Ronald, and Pippa Norris. 2003. The true clash of civilizations. *Foreign Policy*, March, 63–70.

Intergovernmental Panel on Climate Change. 2007. *Climate change 2007: Synthesis report summary for policymakers*. Valencia: Intergovernmental Panel on Climate Change.

International Commission on Intervention and State Sovereignty. 2001. *The responsibility to protect*. Ottawa: International Development Research Centre.

International Monetary Fund. 2006. *Vietnam statistical appendix*. IMF Country Report no. 06/423. Washington, D.C.: International Monetary Fund. http://www.imf.org/external/pubs/ft/scr/2006/cr06423.pdf.

———. 2007. Sub-Saharan Africa: Regional economic outlook. Press release no. 07/237. October 20. http://www.imf.org/external/np/sec/pr/2007/pr07237.htm.

———. 2008. IMF executive directors and voting power. July 3. http://www.imf.org/external/np/sec/memdir/eds.htm.

Isbister, John. 2006. *Promises not kept: Poverty and the betrayal of Third World development*. 7th ed. Bloomfield, Conn.: Kumarian Press.

Ishay, Micheline R. 2004. *The history of human rights from ancient times to the globalization era*. Berkeley and Los Angeles: University of California Press.

Jomo, K. S. 2003. Introduction: Southeast Asia's ersatz miracle. In *Southeast Asian paper tigers? From miracle to debacle and beyond*, ed. K. S. Jomo. New York: Routledge.

Jones, Adam. 2006. *Genocide: A comprehensive introduction*. New York: Routledge.

Jones, Charles. 1999. *Global justice: Defending cosmopolitanism*. New York: Oxford University Press.

Jones, Kent. 2004. *Who's afraid of the WTO?* New York: Oxford University Press.

Judt, Tony. 2005. *Postwar: A history of Europe since 1945.* New York: Penguin Press.

Kanbur, Ravi. 2007. Attacking poverty: What is the value added of a human rights approach? Working paper, Cornell University. February. http://www.people.cornell.edu/pages/sk145.

Kanter, James, and Stephen Castle. 2008. Rising food prices sharpen a European debate. *New York Times,* May 20. http://www.nytimes.com/2008/05/20/business/worldbusiness/20subsidy.html.

Kausikan, Bilahari. 1993. Asia's different standard. *Foreign Policy* 92:24–41.

Keck, Margaret E., and Kathryn Sikkink. 1998. *Activists beyond borders: Advocacy networks in international politics.* Ithaca, N.Y.: Cornell University Press.

Kent, George. 2005a. *Freedom from want: The human right to adequate food.* Washington, D.C.: Georgetown University Press.

———. 2005b. The human rights obligations of intergovernmental organizations. *UN Chronicle Online Edition* 42, no. 3. http://www.un.org/Pubs/chronicle/2005/issue3/0305p32.html.

———. 2008. Global obligations. In *Global obligations for the right to food,* ed. G. Kent. New York: Rowman and Littlefield.

Khanna, Parag. 2008. Waving goodbye to hegemony. *New York Times Magazine,* January 27, 34–67.

Kimenyi, Mwangi S. 1997. *Ethnic diversity, liberty, and the state: The African dilemma.* Cheltenham, U.K.: Edward Elgar.

Kinzer, Stephen. 2008. Life under the Ortegas. *New York Review of Books,* June 12, 60–63.

Kitching, Gavin. 2001. *Seeking social justice through globalization.* University Park: Pennsylvania State University Press.

Klein, Naomi. 2000. *No logo: Taking aim at the brand bullies.* Toronto: Vintage Canada.

Kohut, Andrew, and Richard Wike. 2008. All the world's a stage. *National Interest Online,* May 6. http://www.nationalinterest.org/Article.aspx?id=17502.

Kulipossa, Fidelx Pius. 2006. Mozambique. *IDS Bulletin* 37 (2): 40–52.

Landman, Todd. 2002. Comparative politics and human rights. *Human Rights Quarterly* 24 (4): 890–923.

League of Nations. 1926. Convention to suppress the slave trade and slavery. September 25. http://www.yale.edu/lawweb/avalon/league/lea001.htm.

Legrain, Philippe. 2002. *Open world: The truth about globalisation.* London: Abacus.

Leite, Sergio Pereira. 2001. Human rights and the IMF. *Finance and Development,* December. http://www.imf.org/external/pubs/ft/fandd/2001/12/leite.htm.

Lewis, Robert G. 2008. What food crisis? Global hunger and farmers' woes. *World Policy Journal,* Spring, 29–35.

Li, Quan, and Drew Schaub. 2004. Economic globalization and transnational terrorism: A pooled time-series analysis. *Journal of Conflict Resolution* 48 (2): 230–58.

Lindroos, Anja. 2006. Book reviews. *European Journal of International Law* 17:1038–43.

MacMillan, Margaret. 2003. *Paris 1919: Six months that changed the world.* New York: Random House.

Madison, G. B. 1998. *The political economy of civil society and human rights.* New York: Routledge.

Martin, Nigel T. 2008. The FIM G8 project, 2002–2006: A case analysis of a project to initiate civil society engagement with the G8. In *Critical mass: The emergence of global civil society,* ed. J. W. St. G. Walker and A. S. Thompson. Waterloo, Canada: Wilfrid Laurier University Press.

Marx, Karl. [1867] 1967. *Capital.* Vol. 1. New York: International Publishers.

Marx, Karl, and Friedrich Engels. [1888] 1967. *The communist manifesto.* Harmondsworth, UK: Penguin.

Masina, Lameck. 2008. Fertiliser success stuns Western donors. *African Business,* May, 67.

McCorquodale, Robert, and Richard Fairbrother. 1999. Globalization and human rights. *Human Rights Quarterly* 21 (3): 735–66.

McGrew, Anthony G. 1998. Human rights in a global age: Coming to terms with globalization. In *Human rights fifty years on: A reappraisal,* ed. T. Evans. Manchester: Manchester University Press.

McLuhan, Marshall. 1962. *The Gutenburg galaxy: The making of typographic man.* Toronto: University of Toronto Press.

McNeill, William H. 2008. Globalization: Long term process or new era in human affairs? *New Global Studies* 2 (1): 1–9.

McQueen, Anne Marie. 2008. When pub crawls clash with prayer calls. *Globe and Mail,* July 21, A3.

Mertus, Julie A. 2005. *The United Nations and human rights: A guide for a new era.* New York: Routledge.

Meyer, David S., and Nancy Whittier. 1994. Social movement spillover. *Social Problems* 41 (2): 277–98.

Meyer, Willliam H. 1996. Human rights and MNCs: Theory versus quantitative analysis. *Human Rights Quarterly* 18 (2): 368–97.

Milanovic, Branko. 2002. True world income distribution, 1988 and 1993: First calculation based on household surveys alone. *Economic Journal* 112:51–92.

———. 2005. *Worlds apart: Measuring international and global inequality.* Princeton, N.J.: Princeton University Press.

Miller, Jeffrey B., and Stoyan Tenev. 2007. On the role of government in transition: The experiences of China and Russia compared. *Comparative Economic Studies* 49:543–71.

Milner, Wesley T. 2002. Economic globalization and rights: An empirical analysis. In *Globalization and human rights*, ed. A. Brysk. Berkeley and Los Angeles: University of California Press.

Monshipouri, Mahmood, Claude E. Welch Jr., and Evan T. Kennedy. 2003. Multinational corporations and the ethics of global responsibility: Problems and possibilities. *Human Rights Quarterly* 25 (4): 965–89.

Moore, Barrington, Jr. 1966. *Social origins of dictatorship and democracy: Lord and peasant in the making of the modern world*. Boston: Beacon Press.

Morris, Morris David. 1996. Light in the tunnel: The changing condition of the world's poor. http://www.brown.edu/Administration/News_Bureau/Op-Eds/Morris.html.

Mouelhi, Mia, and Arne Ruckert. 2007. Ownership and participation: The limitations of the poverty reduction strategy approach. *Canadian Journal of Development Studies* 28 (2): 277–92.

Murray, Stephen O., and Will Roscoe. 1997. *Islamic homosexualities: Culture, history, and literature*. New York: New York University Press.

Narveson, Jan. 1999. *Moral matters*. 2nd ed. Peterborough, Canada: Broadview.

Neubeck, Kenneth J. 2006. Welfare racism and human rights. In *Economic rights in Canada and the United States*, ed. R. E. Howard-Hassmann and C. E. Welch Jr. Philadelphia: University of Pennsylvania Press.

New York Times. 2008. Food emergency. May 6. http://www.nytimes.com/2008/05/06/opinion/06tue3.html.

Nickel, James W. 1987. *Making sense of human rights: Philosophical reflections on the Universal Declaration of Human Rights*. Berkeley and Los Angeles: University of California Press.

O'Connell, Paul. 2007. On reconciling irreconcilables: Neo-liberal globalisation and human rights. *Human Rights Law Review* 7 (3): 483–509.

Oloka-Onyango, Joe, and Sylvia Tamale. 1995. "The personal is political," or why women's rights are indeed human rights: An African perspective on international feminism. *Human Rights Quarterly* 17 (4): 691–731.

Organisation for Economic Co-operation and Development. 2007. *OECD-FAO agricultural outlook, 2007–2016*. Paris: OECD and Food and Agriculture Organization of the United Nations. http://www.agri-outlook.org/dataoecd/6/10/38893266.pdf.

Ostry, Sylvia. 2009. The World Trade Organization: System under stress. In *Unsettled legitimacy: Political community, power, and authority in a global era*, ed. S. Bernstein and W. D. Coleman. Vancouver: University of British Columbia Press.

Pangalangan, Raul. 2002. Sweatshops and international labor standards: Globalizing markets, localizing norms. In *Globalization and human rights*, ed. A. Brysk. Berkeley and Los Angeles: University of California Press.

Pew Global Attitudes Project. 2007. *Pew Global Attitudes Project: Spring 2007 survey of forty-seven publics.* http://www.pewglobal.org/reports/pdf/256 topline.pdf.

Pogge, Thomas W. 2002. *World poverty and human rights: Cosmopolitan responsibilities and reforms.* Malden, Mass.: Blackwell Publishing.

Polanyi, Karl. 1944. *The great transformation: The political and economic origins of our time.* Boston: Beacon Press.

Polishchuk, Leonid, and Alexei Savvateev. 2004. Spontaneous (non)emergence of property rights. *Economics of Transition* 12 (1): 103–27.

Price, Richard. 2003. Transnational civil society and advocacy in world politics. *World Politics* 55:579–606.

Prieto-Carron, Marina, Peter Lund-Thomsen, Anita Chan, Ana Muro, and Chandra Bhushan. 2006. Critical perspectives on CSR and development: What we know, what we don't know, and what we need to know. *International Affairs* 82 (5): 977–87.

Pritchard, Kathleen. 1989. Human rights and development: Theory and data. In *Human rights and development: International views*, ed. D. P. Forsythe. London: Macmillan.

Ravallion, Martin. 2003. Have we already met the millennium development goal for poverty? Unpublished paper. http://www.iie.com/publications/papers/ravallion0203.pdf.

Rawls, John 1999. A theory of justice [excerpt]. In *Moral issues in global perspective*, ed. C. M. Koggel. Peterborough, Ontario: Broadview Press.

Richards, David L., and Ronald Gelleny. 2007. Women's status and economic globalization. *International Studies Quarterly* 51 (4): 855–76.

Richmond, Anthony. 1994. *Global apartheid: Refugees, racism, and the new world order.* New York: Oxford University Press.

Robison, Kristopher K., Edward M. Crenshaw, and J. Craig Jenkins. 2006. Ideologies of violence: The social origins of Islamist and Leftist transnational terrorism. *Social Forces* 84 (4): 2009–26.

Rodney, Walter. 1972. *How Europe underdeveloped Africa.* London: Bogle-l'Ouverture Publications.

Rodrik, Dani. 2008. Don't cry for Doha. *Policy Innovations*, August 19. http://www.policyinnovations.org/ideas/commentary/data/000077.

Rorty, Richard. 1993. Human rights, rationality, and sentimentality. In *On human rights: The Oxford Amnesty Lectures, 1993*, ed. S. Shute and S. Hurley. New York: Basic Books.

Roth, Kenneth. 2004. Defending economic, social, and cultural rights: Practical issues faced by an international human rights organization. *Human Rights Quarterly* 26 (1): 63–73.

Rueschemeyer, Dietrich, Evelyne Huber Stephens, and John D. Stephens. 1992. *Capitalist development and democracy*. Chicago: University of Chicago Press.

Ruggie, John. 2007. *Business and human rights: Mapping international standards of responsibility and accountability for corporate acts*. New York: United Nations Human Rights Council. http://www.business-humanrights.org/Documents/SRSG-report-Human-Rights-Council-19-Feb-2007.pdf.

Sachs, Jeffrey D. 2005. *The end of poverty: Economic possibilities for our time*. New York: Penguin Press.

Sala-i-Martin, Xavier. 2002. The world distribution of income (estimated from individual country distributions). NBER Working Paper 8933. May 1. http://papers.nber.org/papers/w8933.pdf.

———. 2005. The world distribution of income: Falling poverty and . . . convergence, period. Unpublished paper, Columbia University. October 9. http://www.columbia.edu/~xs23/papers/pdfs/World_Income_Distribution_QJE.pdf.

Sandbrook, Richard. 2000. Globalization and the limits of neoliberal development doctrine. *Third World Quarterly* 21 (6): 1071–80.

Sandbrook, Richard, Mark Edelman, Patrick Heller, and Judith Teichman. 2007. *Social democracy in the global periphery: Origins, challenges, prospects*. New York: Cambridge University Press.

Sassen, Saskia. 2007. *A sociology of globalization*. New York: W. W. Norton.

Saunders, Peter. 1993. Citizenship in a liberal society. In *Citizenship and social theory*, ed. B. S. Turner. Newbury Park, Calif.: Sage.

Schabas, William A. 1991. The omission of the right to property in the international covenants. *Hague Yearbook of International Law* 4:135–70.

Scholte, Jan Aart. 2002. *Globalization: An introduction*. Basingstoke, U.K.: Palgrave.

Schwab, Peter, and Adamantia Pollis. 2000. Globalization's impact on human rights. In *Human rights: New perspectives, new realities*, ed. P. Schwab and A. Pollis. Boulder, Colo.: Lynne Rienner.

Secretary-General. United Nations. 2005. *In larger freedom: towards development, security and human rights for all*. New York: United Nations. http://www.un.org/largerfreedom/.

Sen, Amartya. 1990. More than 100 million women are missing. *New York Review of Books*, December 20, 61–66.

———. 1999. *Development as freedom*. New York: Alfred A. Knopf.

———. 2006. *Identity and violence: The illusion of destiny.* New York: W. W. Norton.

Sennett, Richard. 1978. *The fall of public man: On the social psychology of capitalism.* New York: Vintage Books.

Shue, Henry. 1980. *Basic rights: Subsistence, affluence, and U.S. foreign policy.* Princeton, N.J.: Princeton University Press.

Singer, Peter. 2004. Outsiders: Our obligations to those beyond our borders. In *The ethics of assistance: Morality and the distant needy,* ed. D. K. Chatterjee. New York: Cambridge University Press.

Skogly, Sigrun I. 1997. Complexities in human rights protection: Actors and rights involved in the Ogoni conflict in Nigeria. *Netherlands Quarterly of Human Rights* 15 (1): 47–60.

Smillie, Ian. 2004. Climb every mountain: Civil society and the conflict diamonds campaign. In *Fighting for human rights,* ed. P. Gready. New York: Routledge.

Smith, Jackie. 2004. The World Social Forum and the challenges of global democracy. *Global Networks* 4 (4): 413–21.

———. 2006a. The World Social Forum: An experiment in global democracy. *Peace Colloquy,* Fall, 14–16.

———. 2006b. Economic globalization and labor rights: Towards global solidarity. *Notre Dame Journal of Law, Ethics, and Public Policy* 20 (2): 873–81.

———. 2009. Contested globalizations: Social movements and the struggle for global democracy. In *Unsettled legitimacy: Political community, power, and authority in a global era,* ed. S. Bernstein and W. D. Coleman. Vancouver: University of British Columbia Press.

Smith, Jackie, Melissa Bolyard, and Anna Ippolito. 1999. Human rights and the global economy: A response to Meyer. *Human Rights Quarterly* 21 (1): 207–19.

Smith, Jackie, Ron Pagnucco, and George A. Lopez. 1998. Globalizing human rights: The work of transnational human rights NGOs in the 1990s. *Human Rights Quarterly* 20 (2): 379–412.

Soros, George. 2002. *On globalization.* New York: PublicAffairs.

Spar, Debora L. 1998. The spotlight and the bottom line: How multinationals export human rights. *Foreign Affairs,* March-April, 7–12.

Stamatopoulou, Elissavet. 1995. Women's rights and the United Nations. In *Women's rights, human rights: International feminist perspectives,* ed. J. Peters and A. Wolper. New York: Routledge.

Steinhardt, Ralph G. 2005. Corporate responsibility and the international law of human rights: The new lex mercatoria. In *Non-state actors and human rights,* ed. P. Alston. New York: Oxford University Press.

Stephens, Carolyn, and Simon Bullock. 2004. Civil society and environmental justice. In *Fighting for human rights,* ed. P. Gready. London: Routledge.

Stiglitz, Joseph E. 2001. Foreword to *The great transformation: The political and economic origins of our time,* by K. Polanyi. Boston: Beacon Press.

———. 2002. *Globalization and its discontents.* New York: W. W. Norton.

———. 2006. *Making globalization work.* New York: W. W. Norton.

———. 2008. A global lesson in market failure. *Globe and Mail,* July 8, A17.

Surk, Barbara. 2008. "Perfect storm" brewing for food riots, UN warns. *Globe and Mail,* April 9, A15.

Teivainen, Teivo. 2002. The World Social Forum and global democratisation: Learning from Porto Alegre. *Third World Quarterly* 23 (4): 621–32.

Thomas, Caroline. 1998. International financial institutions and social and economic human rights: An exploration. In *Human rights fifty years on: A reappraisal,* ed. T. Evans. Manchester: Manchester University Press.

Tomasevski, Katarina. 2006. *Free or fee: 2006 global report.* http://www.katarina tomasevski.com

Toussaint, Eric. 2006. South Korea: The miracle unmasked. *Economic and Political Weekly* 41 (39): 4211–19.

Turner, Bryan S. 2006. *Vulnerability and human rights.* Essays on Human Rights, ed. T. Cushman. University Park: Pennsylvania State University Press.

United Nations. 2007. The Global Compact. http://www.un.org/depts/ptd/global.htm.

United Nations Department of Public Information. 2008. Launching Geneva Lecture Series, Secretary-General says global food crisis chance to address root problems of world's poorest, majority of whom are small farmers. UN Doc. SG/SM/11541. http://www.un.org/News/Press/docs/2008/sgsm11541.doc.htm.

United Nations Development Programme. 1994. *Human development report, 1994.* New York: Oxford University Press.

United Nations General Assembly. [1948] 2006. Convention on the Prevention and Punishment of the Crime of Genocide. Resolution 260 A (III). December 12. In *Basic documents on human rights,* ed. I. Brownlie and G. S. Goodwin-Gill, 283–87. 5th ed. New York: Oxford University Press.

———. 1974. Declaration on the Establishment of a New International Economic Order. Resolution 3201 (S-VI). May 1. http://www.un-documents.net/s6r3201.htm.

———. 1986. Declaration on the Right to Development. Resolution 41/128. December 4. http://www.unhchr.ch/html/menu3/6/74.htm.

———. 2007. United Nations Declaration on the Rights of Indigenous Peoples. Resolution A/RES/61/295. September 13. http://www.un.org/esa/socdev/unpfii/en/drip.html.

United Nations Global Compact Office. 2007. *Annual review: 2007 leaders' summit.* June. New York: UN Global Compact Office. http://www.unglobal compact.org/docs/news_events/8.1/GCAnnualReview2007.pdf.

United Nations Office at Geneva. 2008. History of the League of Nations. http://www.unog.ch/80256EE60057D930/(httpPages)/1247483E6FED 755A80256EF8004FE8FD?OpenDocument.

U.S. Department of State. 2008. The Bretton Woods Conference, 1944. http://www.state.gov/r/pa/ho/time/wwii/98681.htm.

Uvin, Peter. 1998. *Aiding violence: The development enterprise in Rwanda.* West Hartford, Conn.: Kumarian Press.

Vivanco, Jose Miguel, and Daniel Wilkinson. 2008. Hugo Chávez versus human rights. *New York Review of Books,* November 6, 68.

Wallerstein, Immanuel. 1980. *The modern world-system II: Mercantilism and the consolidation of the European world-economy, 1600–1750.* Studies in Social Discontinuity. New York: Academic Press.

———. 2001. America and the world: The Twin Towers as metaphor. Charles R. Lawrence II Memorial Lecture, Brooklyn College, New York, December 5.

Weissbrodt, David. 2006. International law of economic, social, and cultural rights: A U.S. perspective. In *Economic rights in Canada and the United States,* ed. R. E. Howard-Hassmann and C. E. Welch Jr. Philadelphia: University of Pennsylvania Press.

Weissbrodt, David, and Connie de la Vega. 2007. *International human rights law: An introduction.* Philadelphia: University of Pennsylvania Press.

Welch, Claude E., Jr. 1995. *Protecting human rights in Africa: Strategies and roles of non-governmental organizations.* Philadelphia: University of Pennsylvania Press.

Wells, Don. 2008. Legitimizing neoliberal globalization: Corporate-state promotion of international labour standards in the global south. Paper presented at the annual meeting of the American Political Science Association, Boston, August 28–31.

Wells-Dang, Andrew. 2002. Having it both ways. *Foreign Affairs* 81 (4): 180–82.

Werlin, Herbert H. 1994. Ghana and South Korea: Exploring development disparities. An essay in honor of Carl Rosberg. *Journal of Asian and African Studies* 29 (3–4): 205–25.

White House. Office of the Press Secretary. 2004. President Bush signs African Growth and Opportunity Act. http://www.whitehouse.gov/news/releases/2004/07/print/20040713-3.html.

Wiseberg, Laurie S. 1991. Protecting human rights activists and NGOs: What more can be done? *Human Rights Quarterly* 13 (4): 525–44.

World Bank. 2008a. Gross domestic product, 2008. World Development Indicators Database. http://siteresources.worldbank.org/DATASTATISTICS/Resources/GDP.pdf.

———. 2008b. Country classification. http://ppi.worldbank.org/resources/ppi_countryClassification.aspx.

———. 2008c. Malawi, fertilizer subsidies, and the World Bank. http://web.worldbank.org/WBSITE/EXTERNAL/COUNTRIES/AFRICAEXT/MALAWIEXTN/0,,contentMDK:21575335~pagePK:141137~piPK:141127~theSitePK:355870,00.html.

Zaidi, Ali. 2009. Personal communication, January 3.

Zakaria, Fareed. 1994. Culture is destiny: A conversation with Lee Kwan Yew. *Foreign Affairs* 73 (2): 109–26.

Zhang, Mo. 2008. From public to private: The newly enacted Chinese property law and the protection of property rights in China. Temple University Legal Studies Research Paper 2008-39, Temple University Beasley School of Law. http://www.ssrn.com/abstract=1084363.

INDEX

Page numbers in *italics* refer to figures or tables.

BRICSAM (Brazil, Russia, India, China, South Africa, and Mexico), 46
Britain
BP, 68
colonialism by, 8, 85
enclosure movement, 34, 52
industrialization, 3, 11, 33–35, 55, 148
slave trade, 129
tourism, 125
welfare provisions, 55
Buffett, Warren, 106
Burma, 46, 134–35
Bush, George W., 51, 53, 96, 144

Cambodia, 78
Cameroon, food riots in, 76
Canada, 26, 108, 138, 141
capital flows. See hot money
capitalism. See also neoliberal capitalism
anticapitalism, 116, 135–36, 141
authoritarian and democratic models of, 16
beneficiary of globalization, 7–8
civil and political rights with, 62–63
class structures, 67–68, 120–21
communisms transformation to, 13
definition, 7
democracy with, 62, 131
economic crisis (2008–9), 143–45
economic transformation to, 11–14, 33–35
environmental concerns of, 112
human rights in evolution of, 83–85
individualism and, 129
inequities of, 147
no alternative to, 119
poverty and, 101
private property in, 52, 139–40
redistributive policies with, 143
regulation of, 39
target of social movements, 2, 104–5, 114
unregulated, 102
without democracy, 56, 64
Caribbean, 25, 30
Central Asia, 30, 46. See also Asia
Chad-Cameroon oil pipeline, 94
Chávez, Hugo, 136

Chen, Shaohua, 25, 29, 30, 31
children
child labor, 89, 97, 104, 109
education, 41, 60, 109
malnutrition, 76–77, 79
mortality rates, 95, 135
poverty impact on, 124
social movements supporting, 103–4
social roles, 74, 81, 127
Chile, 64, 136, 141–42
China
CSR codes, 92
GDP higher than Toyota, 69
GNI per capita, 20
income compared, 27–28, 28
integration into world economy, 10, 30, 45
international business class, 120
meat consumption, 77
middle-income country, 46
politics of resentment, 115
poverty, 25, 29–30, 31
rule of law, 59
rural-urban inequality, 24, 30
social activism in, 100
as special case, 45
TNCs based in, 69
transition of economy of, 13
UN covenants ratified, 87
workers' rights, 87
Christians, 107–8, 119, 128
Churchill, Winston, 9
Cingranelli, David, 41
Circumpolar Conference, 108
civil and political rights. See also human rights
alienation from lack of, 147
from capitalism, 62–63
definition/terminology, 4–5
economic human rights and, 53–54, 143
in model of globalization/human rights, 57, 60–61
political legitimacy and, 63
civil society. See also social activism and movements
culture of activism, 15–16
definition/terminology, 99–100

in global governance, 109–10
NGOs and, 106, 108–9
civil unrest in food crisis (2008), 76, 81
civil unrest in model of globalization/human
rights, 70, 72
civil wars, 15, 30, 45, 46, 92
Clapham, Andrew, 94, 96
class structure
activism, 63–64
based on rewards, 139
with capitalism, 67–68
compromising with, 142, 143
diasporas in, 120–21
inequity in, 67
international business class, 120
in kin and village-based societies, 74
in models of globalization/human rights,
49, 58–59, 58–60, 61–62, 70, 71
politics of resentment, 118
in pre-capitalist societies, 75
social movements transforming, 101–2
terrorism and, 146
in universal human rights, 110, *111*
coffee in model of food crisis (2008), 78–82
Collier, Paul, 2
colonialism and neocolonialism
antiglobalization in, 147
cultural imperialism as, 148
development dictatorships of, 37
globalization as, 67
lawlessness of, 85
law prohibiting, 84
politics of resentment and, 129
redistribution of wealth and, 132
communism, 10, 13, 141. *See also* socialist and
closed economies
community and sociability
communities of obligation, 122–23
of diasporas, 120–21
inequality in, 140
integralists criticism of West and, 129
loss in model of world food crisis (2008),
78–82, 79
loss of, 34–35, 36, 74–75, 86–87
politics of resentment, 118

social relations disrupted, 13–14, 33–35
social roles in, 122, 124
sustaining through collectivism, 37
through socialism, 134
universe of obligation, 132
Congo, 110
consumerism
consumer campaigns, 91, 103–4, 105–6
culture of consumer goods, 124
politics of resentment, 121–22, 124–26
Convention on the Prevention and Punishment
of the Crime of Genocide, 14
Convention Relating to the Status of
Refugees, 121
corporate social responsibility (CSR) codes,
91–92
corruption in government
in closed economies, 134–35
controlling, 45, 90
developmental dictatorships, 37–38
economic rights to combat, 58–59, 95
property rights to combat, 60, 139
"shock treatment" policies, 30
Costa Rica, 141–42
Cuba, 134–35
Czech Republic, 13

DBCP (pesticides), 89
Declaration of Fundamental Principles and
Rights at Work (ILO), 89–90
Declaration on the Rights of Indigenous
Peoples, 108
Declaration on the Right to Development
(UN), 38
Del Monte Foods, 89, 103
democracy and social democracy. *See also*
national sovereignty; property rights
and private ownership; public policy
accountability, transparency, and good
governance, 47
capitalism connection, 62
as defense from globalization, 5, 137–43
definition of, 137
facilitating, 63–64
human rights with, 2, 15–16, 119

sociability. *See* community and sociability
social activism and movements. *See also* boy-
    cotts; civil society
    in ameliorating poverty, 47–48
    antiglobalization, 2, 104–5, 146–47
    antimarket and anti-Western, 117
    class based, 62, 101–2
    consumer campaigns, 91, 103–4, 105–6
    culture of activism, 15–16
    definition/terminology, 100–101
    effect on globalization, 6
    environmental activism, 105
    feminism, 108
    inequality's effect on, 27
    necessary for human rights, 17, 56, 58,
        62–63, 83
    NGOs and, 106–10
    result of SAPs, 41
    understanding economics, 112–14
    universal human rights, 110, *111*
socialist and closed economies
    communist trade unions, 141
    Cuba, 134–35
    deny market opportunities, 51–52
    free trade to combat, 10
    integrate into world economy, 13
    path to development, 36–38
    Venezuela, 136–37
social networks, 122–23
social relations disrupted, 13–14, 33–35. *See also*
    community and sociability
Somalia, 76
Soros, George, 7, 42
South Africa, 15, 46, 69
South Asian poverty, 25, 29
Southeast Asian economic meltdown, 43, 50, 71
South Korea (Republic of Korea), 12, 39, 56, 69
Soviet Union, 13, 30, 36–37, 46
Spain, 85
Speenhamland Laws (UK), 55
state owned enterprises (SOEs), 40, 88
statistics
    absolute and relative income compared,
        27–28, *28*
    absolute poverty levels, 24–26, *25*

child malnutrition, 76–77
consumption during food crisis, 81–82
food prices in 2008 crisis, 76
Gini coefficient ranges among countries,
    26–27
number of HRNGOs, 100
people living below poverty line, 31
U.S. income ratios, 141
Western foreign aid, 133
world income inequality indexes, 24
of world inequality, 22–23
Stiglitz, Joseph E., 42, 50, 69, 71
structural adjustment programs (SAPs),
    40–42, 73–74, 80–81. *See also* interna-
    tional financial institutes (IFIs)
sub-Saharan Africa. *See also* Africa
    absolute poverty levels, 25
    alienation in, 146–47
    in bottom billion, 46
    inequality range (Gini coefficient), 26
    poverty rates in, 30, 45
    as special case, 45
subsistence rights. *See also* human rights
    free trade in, 44
    loss of, 73, 78, 79, 80–81
    in models of globalization/human
        rights, 55
    security need for, 63
    through socialism, 134
    in urbanization, 75
    workers' movements for, 109, 112
Sudan, 42
Summers, Larry, 113
Summit of the Americas, 104
surveys of household consumption, 21–22, 23,
    25–26, 31
Survival International (NGO), 108

Taiwan, 56
taxation. *See also* redistribution of wealth
    increased revenue from, 44
    in model of food crisis (2008), 79, 80
    in models of globalization/human rights,
        57, 58, 62, 70, 71
    negative income tax, 140